The Art of
Emotional Healing

~~~~~~

OTHER WORKS BY LUCIA CAPACCHIONE

Books

The Creative Journal: The Art of Finding Yourself

The Power of Your Other Hand

The Well-being Journal: Drawing on Your Inner Power to Heal Yourself

The Creative Journal for Children: A Guide for Parents, Teachers, and Counselors

The Creative Journal for Teens

The Creative Journal for Parents

Lighten Up Your Body, Lighten Up Your Life
(with Elizabeth Johnson and James Strohecker)

The Picture of Health: Healing Your Life with Art

Recovery of Your Inner Child

Putting Your Talent to Work (with Peggy Van Pelt)

Visioning: Ten Steps to Designing the Life of Your Dreams

Audio

The Picture of Health: Well-Being Journal Meditations

The Wisdom of Your Other Hand (five tapes on Creative Journal and art therapy, inner family work, body/mind healing, relationship, career)

The Sound of Feelings: Music for Emotional Healing, with Jessie Allen Cooper (Series of 6 CDs with musical accompaniment to the 9 families of feelings presented in the book)

For information regarding materials, public presentations, consultations, and Creative Journal Expressive Arts certification training, contact: Lucia Capacchione at P.O. Box 1355, Cambria, CA 93428 (805) 546-1424, or visit her Web site at: www.luciac.com

The Art of
Emotional Healing

Lucia Capacchione, Ph.D.

SHAMBHALA
Boston & London
2006

SHAMBHALA PUBLICATIONS, INC.
2129 13th Street
Boulder, Colorado 80302
www.shambhala.com

Excerpts from *The Creative Journal: The Art of Finding Yourself* by Lucia Capacchione
are reprinted with permission of Ohio University/Swallow Press, Athens, Ohio.

"The Guest House," from *The Essential Rumi* by Jelaluddin Rumi, translated by
Coleman Barks and John Moyne, originally published by Threshold Books,
is reprinted here with permission.

14 13 12 11 10 9 8

First published in 2001 by Jeremy P. Tarcher/Putnam,
a division of Penguin Putnam Inc., under the title *Living with Feeling*.

Printed in the United States of America

Shambhala Publications makes every effort to print on acid-free, recycled paper.
For more information please visit www.shambhala.com.
Shambhala Publications is distributed worldwide by
Penguin Random House, Inc., and its subsidiaries.

Library of Congress Cataloging-in-Publication Data
Capacchione, Lucia.
[Living with feeling]
The art of emotional healing / by Lucia Capacchione.
p. cm.
Includes bibliographical references.
ISBN 978-1-59030-306-1 (pbk.: alk. paper)
1. Expression. 2. Emotions. I. Title.
BF591.C37 2006
152.4—dc22

THANKS

To the Contributors of artwork and other examples

Felice Bachrach

Christian

Susan Conners

Marsha Nelson, Ph.D.

Lucille Isenberg

Keiko Ishikawa

Pamela Karle

Jeanette Kiess

Jan Meshkoff

Jane Wheeler

D. Anney Zee

To my personal support team

Marsha Nelson, Isela Bezada-Chokr, and Jennifer Star for their dedication
and professional support in helping to take this work to others.
Marilyn Abraham for her enthusiasm and superb editing.

All the certified graduates of my Creative Journal Expressive Arts Program
for their commitment to this work and for teaching me so much
about further applications in the field.

Eden Steinberg, my editor at Shambhala, and her staff.

This book is dedicated to all those who have ever used the arts
for honoring their emotions and for living with feeling.

CONTENTS

Introduction   *1*
The emotional self
Emotions and body-mind medicine
The way of emotions

PART ONE   Embracing Your Emotional Self   9

~~~~~~

1. How Do You Feel?   *11*
   Emotions: what they are and where they come from
   Emotions: what they're good for
   Emotions and the mind
   Emotions and relationships
   Emotional literacy
   Negative emotions: releasing the old ones, dealing with current ones
   Learning the language of feelings
   Nine Families of Feelings
   Meeting your emotional self

2. What Can I Do with My Feelings?   *31*
   Discovering the art of emotional expression
   But I can't draw a straight line
   Emotions and the right brain
   You ought to be in pictures
   The expressive arts
   The arts as process, not product
   Sometimes art happens
   Two brains, two hands: right, left, write
   Facing the critic
   Answering back
   The three brains
   Expressive arts: matching the medium to the mood
   Materials

3. Feelings in Your Body   *52*
   Emotions as energy
   How emotions get stored in your body
   Reclaiming our emotions
   Feeling the body
   What the drawing means
   The body as storyteller

PART TWO   Expressive Your Feelings   *67*

~~~~~~

   The ABCs of feelings: match the medium to the mood
   Directory of emotions: an alphabetical reference guide to emotions

4. The Color of Emotions: From Red with Rage to Feeling Blue   *75*
   The ABCs of drawing: color, line, shape, and texture
   Drawing out your feelings
   Emotions at the boiling point: anger and rage

The image of feelings
The art of collage
Feeling scattered
When nothing makes sense: chaos, confusion, and ambivalence
Exploring pastels
Painting your feelings
Scared stiff: fear
Feeling down: depression, sadness, and grief
Revisiting earlier activities
Helplessness and vulnerability
At home with yourself: happiness, love, and playfulness
Expressive arts as meditation: peace, contentment, and serenity
Embracing happiness: joy, enthusiasm, and creativity
Try a little tenderness: love

5. Sculpted Feelings: Mad, Sad, and Glad   *109*
Preparing the clay, preparing yourself
Comments about the process
The hot emotions: anger, sexuality, and passion
Getting down to earth
Sexuality and sensuality
My body self
Feelings of loss: grief, sadness, and loneliness
Journaling: a handmade life

6. The Sound of Feelings: From Sadness to Joy   *130*
Emotions and sound
Sound as environment
Music as medicine
Journal entry
Music as therapy
Sounds around us
Drumming and the hot emotions
Emotions and vocal sound
Vocalizing our feelings

Sounding our depths: sadness, loneliness, and grief
Toning
Mantra and sound meditation: peace and contentment
A meditative atmosphere
Sounds from the heart: happiness, love, and playfulness
Music for exploring the sound of feelings

7. Emotions in Motion: Moving Your Mood, Dancing for Joy   *153*
Body language and emotions
The Dancer Within
Blocks to spontaneous dance
Moving your feelings out
The work of Gabrielle Roth and the five rhythms
Trance dancing: when the spirit moves you
The inward emotions: sadness, vulnerability, and fear
Nurturing the self: love and self-care
Taking a stand: protectiveness and assertiveness
Outgoing feelings: anger, passion, and sexuality
Movement as spiritual practice: peace and serenity
Roots and wings: joy, playfulness, and creativity
Emotions as energy

PART THREE   Understanding Your Feelings   *173*

∿∿∿∿∿∿∿∿∿∿∿∿∿∿∿∿∿∿∿∿∿∿∿∿∿∿

Insight through words

8. When Your Feelings Tell Their Story, Pay Attention   *177*
In the beginning was the Word
I found it at the movies
Writing from the still image
Writing from feelings
Writing as medicine
Listening to the guide within

9. Facing Ourselves: Mask Making and Inner Dialogues   *192*
   Finding our many selves
   Subpersonalities and emotions
   Mask making and our many selves
   The woman of darkness and light
   Methods of mask making
   Joy, enthusiasm, and playfulness
   Exploring the selves through Voice Dialogue

10. Accepting Your Feelings: Letting Go of Judgment   *210*
    Clearing the emotions by clearing the mind
    A change of mind
    A change of heart: nurturing yourself
    As we believe, so we feel: dropping old baggage
    Clearing old patterns
    Changing your mind about feelings
    Letting your feelings be your guide: changing your life creatively

   Resources   *237*
   Materials
   Sources for art materials and supplies
   Books, audio and video cassettes
   Body charts: chapter three

The Guest House

This being human is a guest house.
Every morning a new arrival.

A joy, a depression, a meanness,
some momentary awareness comes
as an unexpected visitor.

Welcome and entertain them all!
Even if they're a crowd of sorrows,
who violently sweep your house
empty of its furniture,
still, treat each guest honorably.
He may be clearing you out
for some new delight.

The dark thoughts, the shame, the malice,
meet them at the door laughing,
and invite them in.

Be grateful for whoever comes,
because each has been sent
as a guide from beyond.

–JELALUDDIN RUMI *(1207–1273)*
from *The Essential Rumi*, translated by
Coleman Barks and John Moyne

The Art of
Emotional Healing

INTRODUCTION

Who has seen the wind?
Neither you nor I:
But when the trees bow down their heads,
The wind is passing by.

—CHRISTINA ROSSETTI *(1830–1894)*

The emotional self

Like the wind in this old nursery rhyme, emotions are invisible. We can't see them directly with our normal vision. Rather, we *feel* them in our bodies. The same word—*feelings*—describes both physical sensations and emotions. This is no accident. Certainly you have experienced:

- nervousness that gave you *butterflies in your stomach*
- anger that *burned you up*
- fear that *stopped you cold*
- excitement that had you *jumping for joy*

- love and affection that *melted your heart*
- bottled up sadness that left *a lump in your throat*
- relief that felt as if *a weight had been lifted from your shoulders*

As for detecting other people's emotions, you know by the signs. Even when no words are spoken, you often know what's going on inside another person. Sadness shows up in a teardrop, anger in a frown, playfulness in a carefree hand gesture, fear in a jittery foot, happiness in an ear-to-ear grin. When it comes to emotions, body language speaks louder than words. Has anyone ever declared to you, "Who, *me?* Angry? No, I'm not. I'm just fine." Yet the clipped tone and set jaw told a different story. This is the quintessence of incongruity: saying one thing but feeling and thinking something else. Yet you probably were not fooled. The face and voice belie the real truth. Emotions will come out, like it or not.

The Latin roots of the word *emotion* tell the whole tale: *e* (out) + *movere* (move).

Feelings either flow naturally, like a river, or get dammed up. If blocked, they may well up in the subconscious, that subterranean region too deep for the light of awareness to reach. Relegating unwanted emotions to our depths can cause tension headaches or worse. Eventually, these orphaned feelings will leak out, overflow, or burst out in a deluge.

It is the nature of emotions to move. If you want to see for yourself, watch infants and young children. Before they've learned to squelch certain emotions, little kids just let them out. Three-year-old Jana is cuddling her teddy bear when it is abruptly pulled out of her hands by a playmate. Jana howls with anger. Nine-year-old Bobby, upon learning that his pet rabbit has died, immediately bursts into sobs of grief.

Emotions provide motivation to act for our own survival. Tanya learned to fear traffic when she saw a neighborhood dog hit by a car. Her fear keeps her from playing in the street and is therefore life serving.

Emotions also enable us to embrace life with honesty, creativity, and enthusiasm. Feelings enliven us, giving color and texture to our experiences. To feel the full range of emotions is like painting with a complete palette of colors. Ask anyone who has experienced severe or sustained periods of depression. When feelings vanish, and one is emotionally flat, life hardly seems worth living. In fact, this gray state sometimes triggers suicidal thoughts or actions.

From merely surviving to experiencing true vitality, emotions serve us well. However, we need to know what emotions are and what we have to learn from them.

This book is an owner's manual for feeling, accepting, and expressing emotions. The case studies and techniques in it are arranged in sequence. If done in the order presented, the activities herein will lead you to embrace all your emotions in creative and effective ways. In the process, you will learn to *live with feeling*, balancing head and heart, body and soul.

So why do we need another book about emotions? The shelves of libraries and bookstores are filled with self-help books about anger, depression, fear, grief, loneliness, and love. Hasn't there been enough written already? That's a question I always ask when contemplating whether to write a new book. The answer is always the same. In this case, clients, students, and readers have expressed a strong need. Struggling with emotions, they E-mail or call asking for practical tools for living the answers to these big questions:

- How do I find my emotions and really feel them?
- Once I get in touch with them, what do I do with my emotions?
- How do I handle a specific feeling such as fear, loneliness, grief, or rage?

Ah, yes. Emotions. Those messy, irrational, confounding, naughty little tricksters who pop up at the most inopportune moments. Just when you thought you had finished grieving the death of a loved one, tears suddenly start welling up right in the middle of the supermarket. Or you were so certain you had your anger in check, only to have it leap out in a temper tantrum at work, of all places. Suddenly you shrank from a competent professional to an unruly child throwing a fit. How embarrassing, how dangerous. Such outbursts can become even more lethal when they erupt as "road rage" while driving home from work in stop-and-go traffic.

We read about managing our emotions or impulse control. And we try. But what often happens is that we suppress (stuff down) or repress (deny) our unruly feelings. Like the variety of bamboo that spreads through a massive network of underground branching roots, we cut our emotions down here only to have them show up yards away, through the concrete, gravel, and bricks of our life. Where will our hidden feelings pop out next: in the bedroom or at a board meeting? At church or on the way to work?

On the opposite side of the spectrum are the people who couldn't feel an emotion if their lives depended on it. (And the quality of their lives and health do depend on it, I assure you.) What happens to those who have numbed or stuffed their emotions because it's been just too painful, scary, or unacceptable to feel them? Some of these people turn to addictions or medication to sedate their feelings. Others store the emotions in the closets of their bodies and suffer from stress disorders. Remember, emotions will come out, sooner or later. They've got to keep moving.

Emotions and body-mind medicine

Various studies have shown that approximately 80 percent of visits to the doctor are the result of stress-related conditions. And evidence is mounting that many illnesses are simply cries for help with emotions. Research into support groups, body-mind counseling, meditation, expressive arts therapy, biofeedback, and other psychospiritual treatment methods shows that many patients improve, go into remission, or live longer than control groups. This line of inquiry is not new. In the 1970s Dr. Hans Selye, in his book *The Stress of Life,* and Kenneth Pelletier, in *Mind as Healer, Mind as Slayer,* mapped out the territory. Dr. Herbert Benson of Harvard provided practical guidance in his book *The Relaxation Response,* and in the '80s, Benson's associate, Dr. Joan Borysenko, expanded upon meditation and relaxation techniques in her book *Minding the Body, Mending the Mind.*

By the '90s, our understanding of how thoughts and emotions affect our bodies, and vice versa, had grown by leaps and bounds. As an art therapist and leader of health support groups, in the late '80s and early '90s I published several books on body-mind healing and recovery through the arts. I was grateful for support and endorsements from Dr. Borysenko, Dr. Bernie Siegel (oncologist and author of *Love, Medicine and Miracles*), Norman Cousins (who laughed himself well), and Dr. James Pennebaker, whose research into the healing power of writing has corroborated my own findings.

In the last decade, so-called alternative or body-mind medicine, once considered fringy and faddish by the medical establishment, has gradually moved toward the mainstream. Big pharmaceutical companies are advertising their own line of herbal remedies on television. Ten years ago, such potions were still considered the domain of quacks or witches. Of course, they still are in some quarters, but the tide is clearly shifting by popular demand. Polls and studies indicate that one in three Americans are turning to remedies and treatments of alternative or holistic medicine: chiropractic, acupuncture, body-mind therapies, biofeedback, hypnotherapy, naturopathic medicine, and homeopathy. Some health insurance companies, having recognized the dollar-saving value of these approaches, are now covering such things as chiropractic and acupuncture.

Reputable physicians like Bernie Siegel and Larry Dossey even talk about prayer as medicine and cite data from hard science complete with replicable control-group studies. It's getting more and more difficult to pooh-pooh these experienced clinicians and researchers as oddballs. Judging from the popularity of authors and speakers like physician Deepak Chopra, who has popularized the ancient Indian art of ayurvedic medicine, and Dr. Christiane Northrup, who brings compassion and common sense to women's medicine, the public is listening with all ears. In later chapters, you'll read about the latest work being done in writing, music, and art as medicine. You'll also learn more about my own clinical experiences with spontaneous healings that have resulted from art and journal writing.

The research of psychologist Dr. James Pennebaker and others has shown that writing about one's illness actually boosts one's immunity. When we met and compared notes in the late '80s, Pennebaker immediately recognized the value of my Creative Journal method. Although he hadn't included drawing in his published research projects, Pennebaker suggested that the spontaneous healing I was seeing with my clients and students was rooted in the same premise he was working with: Emotional expression is healing. The work of physician Dr. Alfred Tomatis (discoverer of the Mozart effect) is attracting the attention of laypeople as well as health professionals. The medical prescription of tomorrow may be "Listen to this sonata and call me in the morning." In Chapter Three you'll read the case study of one of my journal students, Lucille, who healed herself through a written dialogue. In a reversal of roles, this spunky patient informed her skeptical physician that she wanted to postpone exploratory surgery for a chronic condition so that she could first write a conversation with the body part in question. After Lucille's body chat, the symptoms disappeared, never to return. Much to the doctor's surprise, surgery of any kind (exploratory or otherwise) became unnecessary.

One of the most respected researchers in body-mind science is Dr. Candace B. Pert, researcher/professor in the Department of Biophysics and Physiology at Georgetown University. In her groundbreaking book, *Molecules of Emotion: Why You Feel the Way You Feel,* Dr. Pert makes a strong case for the healthy expression of our true feelings. She has found that if the outward expression does not match the inner emotion being felt—in other words, if a person is being incongruent—a conflict is set up in the body that drains energy away from the vital organs. In her book, she writes:

> My research has shown me that when emotions are expressed—which is to say that the biochemicals that are the substrate of emotion are flowing freely—all systems are united and made whole. When emotions are repressed, denied, not allowed to be whatever they may be, our network pathways get blocked, stopping the flow of the vital feel-good unifying chemicals that run both our biology and our behavior. This, I believe, is the state of unhealed feeling we want so desperately to escape from. Drugs, legal or illegal, are further interrupting the many feedback loops that allow the psychosomatic network to function in a natural balanced way, and therefore setting up conditions for somatic as well as mental disorders.

The way of emotions

Emotions move through us when they are accepted and expressed. When this happens, feelings enliven us and fuel our creativity. This book provides activities for allowing your feelings to live and breathe. Based on the laboratory of my own life experience, coupled with more than twenty-five years of clinical practice, teaching, and correspondence with readers, I have designed activities for experiencing emotions directly through expressive arts media. These include drawing, painting, collage, clay, music, movement, writing, mask making, and dramatic dialogues. I hasten to add that you don't have to be talented or skilled in the arts to use these materials. If expressing yourself in the arts terrifies you, you'll receive guidance through these obstacles in Chapter Two.

For now let me just assure you that, unlike the performing and exhibition arts, expressive arts serve primarily as a road into feelings. You will not be critiqued or asked to show your work to anyone else. The only critic you'll meet is the one inside.

Through these activities, which I think of as creative experiments, you will attempt to answer, for yourself, the most common questions asked about emotions:

- How to find and feel emotions
- What to do with difficult, strong, or overpowering feelings once they've been uncovered

Although I have years of experience, credentials, and publications to my credit, to be honest these are a small part of my qualifications for writing this book. The truth is that I have struggled with feelings all my life. Like you, I have been in the fray, not sequestered in an ivory tower analyzing or theorizing about emotions. I come to these questions, first and foremost, as a human being who has lived, loved, hated, grieved, doubted, hoped, feared, felt depression and bliss and all the rest. In other words, I have been around the emotional block a few times. If that weren't enough, I come from southern California (the capital of touchy-feely therapies) and spent my young adult-hood in the '60s and '70s sorting out feelings from thoughts, and beliefs from experience, like a kindergartner classifying colors and shapes. It was de rigueur in the neighborhood where I lived.

I've asked all the same questions you do, hoping "to live along some distant day into the answer," as poet Rainer Maria Rilke put it. Along the way there have been scores of successes and failures, gut-wrenching disappointments as well as huge dreams come true. Although I am inherently an artist, I have discovered that there is much science in art (curiosity, discipline, honest observation, and pragmatism). And there is an art to being a therapist. The laboratory where I cooked up most of the activities in this book was my own journal and my art therapy practice. These creative experiments came to me while engaged in my own personal process or while guiding clients in the experience of art for personal growth and healing. As in scientific research, these creative experiments are replicable and have yielded similar results for readers as well as therapists who have applied my methods with their clients. Here is some feedback from those who have used this process. Perhaps some of these results are ones you also seek.

- I am more in touch with emotions and with body sensations.
- I can access and feel emotions stored in my body as psychosomatic symptoms.
- I have had firsthand experiences of the Inner Child, its feelings and needs.
- I can recognize and name feelings now.
- I can communicate feelings to others in nonthreatening ways.
- I am finding talent I didn't know I had and am using it in all areas of life.

As you engage in these creative experiments, remember they are offered to you in a spirit of see-for-yourself. Call it art, call it science. The name doesn't matter, the *process* does. Personal experience is the best and only guide worth studying. Good teachers are door openers into that wisdom you already have inside—wisdom you can only know through firsthand experience. So let me open the door to the experience and expression of your own emotions: the path to finding your own truth.

PART ONE

Embracing Your Emotional Self

1. HOW DO YOU FEEL?

Emotions: what they are
and where they come from

An old tale from India tells of a man who encounters a snake while walking on a dimly lit road at dusk. He is frozen with fear until someone comes along and points out that the "snake" is only a coiled rope left by the roadside. In an instant, the man's panic turns to relief. This story is told to spiritual seekers to teach an important principle: The world is as you see it.

Emotions are our response to experience. In Webster's dictionary, *emotions* are defined as:

- strong feeling; excitement
- the state or capability of having the feelings aroused to the point of awareness
- any specific feeling; any of various complex reactions with both mental and physical manifestations, as love, hate fear, anger, etc.

Like all of our inner experiences, emotions come from us. That's why we say we *have* emotions. Emotions are our response to the world around us, but also to our thoughts, beliefs, and to our own imaginings. We often say that so-and-so made us angry, but the truth is that no one and no thing outside make us feel anything. We respond to our own perceptions of the world.

The car breaks down, and you get *annoyed* about the inconvenience. You have it towed to the garage for diagnosis. Then you start *fretting* about how much the repair will cost. Will it be major surgery? You're informed that it's only a minor repair. "Whew, what a *relief*," you sigh.

An old and dear friend calls. You're *happy* to hear from her, until she tells you her mother was suddenly taken seriously ill. *Shock* and then *sadness* set in. You feel *compassion* and offer any help you can give.

And so it goes throughout the day, one emotion following after another. Some feelings hang around longer, like grief over the death of a loved one, while others pass in a minute. Some days are more emotionally intense than others. Some periods of life seem like a prolonged stormy season, with one turbulent event after another. Other times are characterized by calm and contentment. One thing is for sure: To be human is to have feelings.

How we perceive life in general also determines how we feel. Some people see the whole world as if it were a snake ready to pounce. They are plagued with chronic fear and anxiety. Do you know any people like that? Others seem to feel little or nothing at all. Lacking emotional responsiveness, they cannot communicate what's going on with them. Are there any people like this in your life? Then there are those who see every experience as an opportunity, a stepping-stone toward growth and aliveness. They are married to life, for better or for worse, taking the bitter with the sweet. I suspect that most people live somewhere in between, surfing the waves of emotions that pass through each day.

Just as perception influences feelings, feelings also shape our experiences. If we're in a bad mood, someone whistling nearby may seem like a nuisance. On the other hand, if we're already feeling cheerful we might join in and whistle along. Emotions are also driven by what we *believe*. For example, we each learn to fear certain things. Everyone has their own list: speaking in public, death, snakes, tornadoes, financial losses, spiders, cops, strangers, being abandoned by loved ones. The list goes on.

Stop for a moment. Get some paper and a pen and make a list of all the things and categories of people you fear. Next to each one, write down why you are afraid of that item or type of person.

Then make a list of your favorite things (that includes people, places, and experiences). After each item, write down the *feeling* it evokes in you.

Emotions: what they're good for

Why do we have emotions? What are they good for? For one thing, emotions have helped you survive. When you were growing up, if you didn't feel fear, you could have gotten hurt. One woman said that during the psychedelic 1960s, while in a drug-induced altered state, she felt absolute fearlessness. Under the impression that she was invincible and could fly, this young woman walked off a cliff and was nearly killed.

Another woman used anger to *save* her life. After years of being battered physically and emotionally by an alcoholic husband, she sought refuge in a women's shelter. With some therapy, she learned to turn down the volume on her fear and let her rage speak.

Getting in touch with some righteous anger empowered her to get out and stay out of this destructive relationship. In this case she traded the fear and intimidation that had crippled her for an active emotion: anger. The turning point came when she used her anger to fuel some constructive action. Through journaling, she has felt and faced her emotions: anger, resentment, grief, and more. Reconciliation is out of the question, however, because her husband has continued to drink and have violent outbursts. She is unwilling to go back for more abuse. By expanding her repertoire of emotions, instead of staying frozen in fear, she is building a new life for herself.

Survival depends on our instinctual and emotional responses. It's easy to see how anger and fear can save lives. But what about the other emotions, like happiness, playfulness, love, and peace? They grace us with the joyful side of life. These emotions have even been shown to strengthen our immune system and contribute to a sense of well-being. We need to experience the whole spectrum in order to be fully human. Emotions open us up to ourselves, each other, and our own interpretation of the divine. Prayers of supplication come from the depths of pain, like Job's. Thanksgiving often comes from the heights of ecstasy, like St. Francis of Assisi's celebration of God in nature, in his poem "The Canticle of Brother Sun."

Emotions are important indicators of our wellness. Often problems arise from the expectation that we should feel good all the time, and if we don't we're not measuring up. "Cheer up," people say to the person who looks sad. "Calm down," they say to the person who is expressing anger. And to the person who shares feelings of apprehension they say, "There's nothing to fear." In all these cases, the feeling person's emotions are being denied and denigrated. That is not to say that the other extreme—staying stuck in certain emotions, such as depression or chronic rage—is the answer. Quite the contrary, either end of the spectrum presents problems. Either the absence of feelings or being chronically overwhelmed by emotions contributes to a life that is out of balance, impacting one's work, relationships, health, and more.

This book is about accepting all of our feelings. It is an antidote to the customary habit of condemning some emotions as negative (fear, anger, sadness, depression, or confusion) and covering them up with a happy face. The only way out of difficult emotions is through them. Then we can genuinely be receptive to the more pleasant ones (happiness, love, playfulness, and peace).

Emotions and the mind

Emotions create dynamic, physical sensations. Without a body, how would we *feel* our emotions, or anything else for that matter? Yet emotional reactions are also linked to the mind. In the darkened movie theater, for instance, it becomes quite obvious that thoughts manufacture feelings. Some scenes scare, sadden, or arouse us. We know a film is not real life, that the situation we're witnessing was scripted and filmed, but our body and emotions react as if we were personally involved in the action on the screen. We scream, our palms get sweaty, we grab the armrest, close our eyes, laugh, cry, yell, and cheer. As a preschooler, I was taken to see the animated film *Bambi*. When Bambi's mother was killed by hunters, I burst into tears, jumped out of my seat, and escaped up the aisle. I wasn't sitting still for any more of that. This only shows how hooked I was, a true believer in the world of fantasy right from the start. Paradoxically, in spite of this rocky beginning I eventually became a devotee of cinema and of art. And yes, I still cry at the sad scenes.

Emotions and relationships

In relating to others we listen as much for feelings as we do for content. People often speak to us in words, but what they *feel* is conveyed through body language, inflection, and tone. What is said and what is felt may not be the same at all. Robert McKee, the screenwriting guru and author of the book *Story Structure,* has for many years taught an internationally famous course for film and television professionals. He spends one day analyzing the classic *Casablanca,* stopping scene by scene to discuss plot, character development, and the craft of storytelling through pictures. Nowhere have I seen anyone present the principle of incongruence in communication as graphically and clearly as McKee does. *Casablanca* is a wonderful film to rent and study if you want to practice looking for the real emotions underneath the dialogue. One excellent example occurs early in the film. Watch the seemingly polite interchange between the French police official, played by Claude Rains, and the German military officers. This was World War II, when the French and Germans were enemies. Rains's face, body language, and double entendres work together to successfully mask his deep animosity for the Nazi soldiers.

In *Remains of the Day,* we saw Emma Thompson's character hiding her feelings of love for a man who could not show his feelings. But the camera sees right past the words into the human heart. All is revealed through the face, the silences, the body.

Actually, we encounter incongruity all the time, conscious of it or not. In daily face-to-face conversations, we read emotions in posture, gestures, and vocal inflections. They register on our inner eye and ear. On the phone, we listen for subtle nuances of tone, pauses here and an emphasis there. We also read between the lines of letters and E-mail we receive, studying what is not said as much as what is. Our emotion radar doesn't always pick up every feeling being broadcast. We sometimes misinterpret some cues, and others just fly right past us. Yet, in order to get very far in life, we have to understand the language of emotions—the subtext of all human communication—to some degree or another.

Emotional literacy

In scientific circles, there is exciting new brain and behavioral research that gives us a fresh perspective on the role of emotions in our lives. Some studies indicate that whether or not a person leads a fulfilled life depends more on emotional aptitude (motivation, impulse control, and people skills) than it does on traditional measures of intelligence or academic achievement. Daniel Goleman discusses the research in his books, *Emotional Intelligence* and *Working with Emotional Intelligence.* He points out that having a high IQ or many years of schooling has little bearing on emotional health and life fulfillment. Citing groundbreaking research, Goleman discusses the factors at work when individuals with high IQs seem to lose their way in life while those with average IQs excel in their chosen field. The difference seems to revolve around emotional intelligence. He makes it clear that emotional intelligence and IQ are not opposed, but they are different. Furthermore, traditional intelligence tests have lacked any measure for such keys to success as self-discipline, self-awareness, and self-efficacy (the belief that one has mastery over the events of one's life and can meet life's challenges as they arise). The research and ideas in Goleman's books are now being applied in corporations and schools.

If you are an educator or parent, you will probably want to know about a school curriculum entitled Healthy Relationships: A Violence-Prevention Curriculum. Proven effective in many school districts in Canada and the United States, this program was brought to my attention as I began writing this book. I had conversations with Andrew Safer, a member of Men for Change, the Halifax-based community group that developed the program. Numbering about a dozen or so over the years, the group represents a variety of professions: education, social work, traditional medicine, alternative health, economic development, administration, journalism, and communication. Many of them are parents or employed in jobs working with youth and were motivated by concern over the increase in violence in society, especially among young people. Working in partnership with the Halifax County–Bedford District School Board of Nova Scotia, they created fifty-three classroom activities designed for social and psychological development in grades seven through nine. The material has proven highly successful with older teens as well.

A three-year study was conducted with students grades seven through nine in Winnipeg, Manitoba, using 1,143 children. The control group, which did not go through this curriculum, showed little to no improvement. By contrast, students who were in the Healthy Relationships program group showed a decrease in violent behavior and an increase in emotional intelligence, self-esteem, and self-efficacy. The Healthy Relationships program is being used in every Canadian province and territory and has been introduced in thirty-five states in the United States. In addition to public schools, it is also being used in women's shelters, social welfare agencies, and detention, youth, and counseling centers. For more information on this program, see Resources.

Negative emotions: releasing the old ones, dealing with current ones

There are some general categories of emotions whose expression seems to be discouraged in our majority culture, such as anger, sadness, and fear. These have been singled out and seen as taboo. In childhood, we learned that the open expression of one or another of these feelings led to reprimands, ridicule, or punishment. These emotions are labeled as bad, and we assume we are bad for having and expressing them. When emotions are pushed underground they tend to explode suddenly in violent acting out, or they implode in the form of depression, anxiety attacks, stress, or physical illness.

What happens to our orphaned emotions? Where do they go? Where do they hide? One place is in the body. A co-worker seen as troublesome literally becomes our *pain in the neck*. We refer to a bothersome family member as a *headache*. We say we *can't stomach* a neighbor's behavior. Actually we give ourselves a pain in the neck or a headache or a stomachache when we can't *speak our mind* or *get it off our chest*.

Another place we hide our feelings is in our unconscious. A child who isn't allowed to express a certain feeling concludes, "Why feel it in the first place?" After all, the unwanted feeling is only causing trouble, spankings, ridicule, or rejection of one sort or another.

The child may have needed to hide unacceptable feelings from self and others in order to survive, but the adult self can go back and rewrite the script. We can give the emotional self permission to feel and express. But, even as adults, we are often blocked from doing this by pervasive attitudes about emotions. For instance, I encounter many psychologists, spiritual seekers, and religious people who describe anger, fear, sadness, and the like as negative emotions. The word *negative* says everything about their attitude toward these feelings. Some think they are less than spiritual if they get angry. They try to remove the feelings with positive affirmations. Or they might try to force a false forgiveness that is not genuinely felt. I call this "putting whipped cream on a can of worms." It's just another form of suppression and repression.

How do we develop what has been called emotional literacy? How do we learn to read and speak the language of feelings, our own as well as the feelings of others? My approach is to accept feelings and learn from them. But in order to do this, we must learn the language of feelings. It is the language of the Inner Child, the body, the Inner Artist, and the soul. It is the language of intimacy, our deepest communication with ourselves and with others. Once learned, this language can take us to our highest wisdom and our greatest creativity.

Learning the language of feelings

This book is a course in hands-on expressive arts techniques for learning and mastering the language of feelings. It is simple enough to be used by adolescents yet comprehensive enough to be effective for adults. It offers activities suited for both right-brain (nonverbal) and left-brain (verbal) learners. It integrates two- and three-dimensional expressive arts activities, such as

- drawing, painting, and collage making
- modeling with clay
- sound making and music
- movement and dance
- mask making

- dramatic dialogues with subpersonalities
- self-reflective writing in a journal

Some materials and media lend themselves very naturally to the expression of certain emotions. For instance, pounding and modeling with clay is great for releasing anger and strong emotions, and so is drumming. The activities presented in Part Two are matched to certain feelings. In addition there is a directory of emotions with page number references for those wishing to concentrate on a particular set of feelings.

Nine Families of Feelings

In order to simplify and navigate the world of emotions, I have found it useful to group them into clusters, or what I call Families of Feelings. In the diagrams that follow, the general categories of feelings have been captioned as follows:

Happy	Afraid	Confused
Sad	Playful	Depressed
Angry	Loving	Peaceful

Around these emotions, other words that mean the same or similar feelings have been placed in a circular pattern.

As you read these charts, try writing down some of your own words or slang phrases that express each of the core emotion words. You might even want to create your own diagrams like the ones shown in the following pages.

the boys having a good time

blissful

joyful   delighted

grateful   *happy*   enthusiastic

gleeful   excited

glad

melancholy *wrapped around itself*

discouraged

melancholy

disheartened

lonely sad down

hurt

gloomy

grieving

agitated

resentful   bitter

mad   *angry*   enraged

irritated   exasperated

furious

FEAR

anxious

fearful

terrified

horrified

afraid

shaky

nervous

scared

panicked

adventurous

whimsical childlike

spontaneous *playful* creative

lively free

lighthearted

affectionate

warm   compassionate

trusting   *loving*   friendly

tender   kind

nurturing

ambivalent

uneasy   bewildered

troubled   *confused*   conflicted

torn   hesitant

perplexed

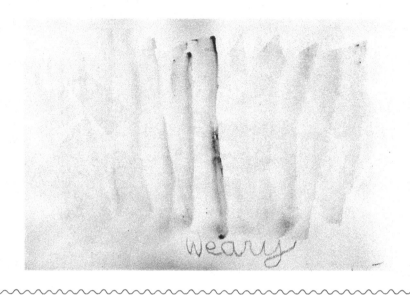

weary

burned out

withdrawn   dejected

weary   ***depressed***   despondent

listless   helpless

hopeless

calm

tranquil   contented

peaceful

serene   relaxed

satisfied   quiet

Meeting your emotional self

As a warm-up for Chapter Two, let's try an exercise to begin your journey of recognizing feelings and expressing emotions.

Feelings

Get some paper and a pen and scribble or doodle the answer to this question: How do you feel right now?

There is no right or wrong way to do this. I'm not asking you to make Art. This is more like the kind of absentminded doodling people do while talking on the phone. Let yourself be a little kid again, making marks on paper. See what happens. Observe how you feel while you're doodling. How do you feel afterward?

Write some feeling words on or around your scribble. If you can't think of any, refer to the Families of Feelings diagrams on the previous pages.

2. WHAT CAN I DO WITH MY FEELINGS?

Discovering the art of emotional expression

I discovered the healing power of getting in touch with feelings while struggling with a serious illness many years ago. My condition defied medical diagnosis or treatment and I seemed to be getting sicker by the day. Lab test mix-ups and errors in prescriptions made matters worse. Realizing that these particular doctors had no answers for me and that they were beginning to be part of the problem, I turned in desperation to my sketch pad. Without realizing what I was doing or where it would lead, I scribbled and doodled my feelings out on paper. These strange drawings scared and puzzled me. I had a degree in art and had worked as a professional designer and artist for years, but these drawings didn't look like any art I'd ever done. The posters, greeting cards, and

banner designs I had created for Hallmark and other companies had been anything but mysterious. They had been bold, colorful, and decorative. There was nothing to interpret.

By contrast, these spontaneous drawings seemed oddly primitive, reflecting none of the technical skill I had achieved as a professional artist. I didn't understand them. In one felt-pen sketch, a little girl crouches under the ground, her tears watering the earth beneath a giant heart-tree that has been split asunder as if by lightning. A dark rain cloud looms above on the left, while two butterflies emerge on the right. Without intending to, I had portrayed the preceding five years of my life (separation, divorce, breakup of business partnership), the present (financial struggles, single parenting, illness, grieving) and the future (rebirth and a new life). I didn't realize any of this at the time.

While creating these drawings, it felt as if my hand had taken over and was doing all the work. My conscious mind had stepped aside; it was like dreaming on paper. I had tapped into the same place we visit in our sleep. Am I losing my mind? I wondered: This looks like the art of mental patients I saw on a college field trip to a psychiatric ward. My drawings made no sense to me; they were like books written in a foreign tongue. Had I really drawn them? What did they mean? Like Alice in Wonderland, I had unwittingly fallen into a mysterious subterranean realm in which all the rules had changed. Yet I always felt better after doing these sketches, so I kept drawing.

What *didn't* feel good was going to the medical clinic for test after test, getting confusing diagnostic results and hit-or-miss treatments. After still another lab error, my patience ran out. One day, out of sheer frustration, I ran to my medicine cabinet and dumped all the capsules and pills in the trash, many of which had caused terrible side effects. I never returned to the HMO. There had to be another way. I didn't know what it was yet, but I knew this wasn't working. Many years later, after I had completely recovered, my condition was diagnosed by an expert in iridology and sclerology, an ancient method of reading markings in the eyes for past and current health problems. I was told I'd had a disorder of the connective tissue or collagen. My life had fallen apart, I had *come unglued.* But I had also put myself back together.

I started sharing my journal drawings and writings with a couple of close friends and co-workers. One of them was Sally, an avid journal keeper who urged me to take my drawings and writings seriously, especially the notes on dreams I was having. I also found my way to some practitioners of holistic health care, a physician who practiced preventive medicine and a nurse trained in bodywork that combined acupressure and massage. My first session with the nurse, Louise, turned into a literal reenactment of a healing dream I'd recently recorded in my journal. In that dream a woman dressed in a doctor's white coat held and comforted me, saying that she knew I was afraid of dying. She also assured me that everything would be all right. I felt as relieved after my first session with Louise as I had upon waking from that dream. Something truly miraculous was happening in realms that I had never explored. Dreams, drawings, stream-of-consciousness writing, precognitive imagery were all blending with waking reality. I was beginning to feel again; my emotions were thawing out of the deep freeze. By recognizing my feelings, I was coming back to life.

At just the right moment another friend suggested a local therapist named Bond Wright. The significance of her name did not escape me. I had fallen apart and needed to put myself back together again. At the mention of her name something deep inside said "Yes!" It was Bond who opened still another door into my emotional and creative self, using an eclectic blend of transactional analysis (often referred to as TA), Gestalt therapy, and neo-Reichian energy work. When Bond and I entered the magical world of therapy, I was directed to hold certain physical postures until my energy started moving on its own. As my body started to vibrate with surges of renewed life force, I saw powerful images in my mind's eye, such as a bottle blowing its cork with emotions gushing out like a geyser. Never had my feelings been allowed to express themselves with such purity and directness. I felt an immediate relief after each of these sessions, and the images and insights I had there always got translated into journal drawings.

At the end of one session Bond sat me down on the floor with a large pad of newsprint and a huge kindergarten crayon. She wanted me to write how I would apply these insights to my everyday life. There was only one catch. She insisted that I write with my nondominant hand, which for me is the left hand. This seemed odd, and I wasn't at all sure I could do it. Little did I know that I was about to do something that would transform my life completely and irrevocably. Here is what I scrawled in huge, awkward letters:

GIVE MYSELF
PERMISSION
TO LET MY CHILD OUT
AND FEEL MY
FEELINGS AND
SAY I'M OKAY!!

As I sat like a young child on the floor struggling to form each letter on the page, the words came out of my mouth spontaneously with the same lisp and tone of voice I'd had during my preschool years. Bond later told me she wished she'd had a videotape of the session. I'd regressed to about four or five years old. That's exactly how old

I had felt while slowly printing on the paper. She explained that this was the point: to give me a firsthand experience of the Feeling Child who was inside me. Buried, perhaps, but still alive. It worked.

I left that session floating, as if a giant weight had been lifted from my shoulders. It had taken huge amounts of energy to keep those emotions stuffed down for thirty-five years. No wonder I had gotten sick. Now they were pouring out, and I was feeling a lightheartedness and effervescence I had never known. At times it was scary but also exhilarating. The more I followed my own advice and gave myself permission to feel and to express my emotions creatively through drawing and writing, the better I felt physically. In three months of weekly sessions with Bond, my goal had been reached: full recovery of my health. Most important, I had come home to my true self: the person I was meant to be.

My heart then prompted me to explore the expressive arts therapies. Working with pioneering art therapist Tobe Reisel for several months led naturally into a new life and new career in art therapy. In my ongoing studies of art for healing, I realized many dreams that had been dormant since childhood: the wish to study dance and movement, to sculpt with clay, to act in improvisational theater, to write and to publish.

But I can't draw a straight line

But what if you're not already an artist, musician, dancer, writer, or actress? How can you be expected to use the arts to feel and express your emotions? The fact is that you *are* an artist, you just don't know it yet. The arts are our natural birthright. That is, until someone tells us we're tone deaf, or have two left feet, or have no artistic talent, and on and on. Let me show you how this happens in just one area: visual art.

The visual image precedes spoken and written language. We think, dream, remember, and imagine the future in pictures. Before there was written language, there were cave paintings. Before children learn to write, they draw. No one had to teach us to draw when we were little kids. They put a pencil or crayon in our hands, gave us a piece of paper, and we started. From scribbles we graduated to amoebalike shapes, straight lines, and dots. Later our markings stood for something: a circle with two dots for eyes and a line for a mouth was labeled Mommy or Grandpa. Then some sticks for legs and arms appeared. Studies have shown that young children all over the world draw the same images and abstract designs. They seem to be using a universal language.

Then it all stops. In literate cultures, school appears to be the dividing line. Once we enter the atmosphere of grades, evaluation, and judgment, the natural artist inside takes a backseat. As we are ushered into the world of ABCs and 123s, the straight lines, circles, and dots become letters and numerals and line up to report for duty to the left brain, where our language centers reside. And the right brain, which specializes in visual-spatial perception, emotional expression, and intuition starts to shrivel up from lack of use. We know that the left brain of adults weighs more than its twin on the right. Another way to observe the atrophy of the right brain is to watch some kids for yourself. You'll never hear preschoolers say they don't have any talent. They don't even know what the word means. They just draw and paint and role-play with costumes and dance and sing as naturally as they run and play and breathe. However, by the time they approach adolescence, you'll hear lots of responses like "I can't" and "No way" when they are asked to express themselves in the arts. By adulthood, the inner artist is on permanent leave of absence in most people.

There are exceptions, of course. Some youngsters have parents who value the arts and provide their children with opportunities to express through these media. Then there are the students who are identified as gifted and qualify for special classes. A small number of innovative schools and teachers use art as an integral part of the curriculum, but these are the exceptions, not the rule. And when art is included in education, it is usually the product that is held in high esteem, not the process. Grades, critiques, and competition abound.

As for the *process* approach, expressive arts are sometimes used as therapy with disturbed, learning disabled, or physically challenged children or with youngsters in crisis (the at-risk kids and those labeled delinquent). Yet almost nowhere do we see expressive arts introduced as a life-skill tool for the average or high-achieving student. I've talked with hundreds of teachers and parents in the United States and Canada. Almost all of them report that in their school districts the arts are still considered stepchildren in the curriculum, and expressive arts emphasizing process and emotional release are rare indeed.

Emotions and the right brain

In prizing the product over the process, we've lost an important part of our instinctual, intuitive way of knowing. In "civilizing" our children with predominantly left-brain techniques that stress language, math, and sequential logic, we shortchange the other half of the brain. I'm referring to the complex set of functions associated with the right cerebral hemisphere: visual and spatial perception, emotional expressiveness, intuitive breakthrough thinking, nonverbal communication, and metaphoric symbolic processing. As a therapist and artist, I know that neglecting the nonverbal language of the right brain leaves us emotionally illiterate. If you really want to understand the price we've paid for our imbalanced reverence for logic and linear thought, read Leonard Shlain's fascinating book, *The Alphabet Versus the Goddess*. Both Shlain's book and Goleman's work on emotional intelligence corroborate my professional experience. In my private practice, I have repeatedly observed the following equation:

training and high IQ + emotional illiteracy   =   burnout
 stress disorders
 depression
 dysfunctional relationships
 unsatisfying careers
 addictions
 violence to self or others

Fortunately, the ability to learn the language of feelings is innate in humans. You can recover it, no matter how old you are. And that's what the activities in this book are designed to do: help you reclaim your feelings and the ability to express them.

You ought to be in pictures

In using the expressive arts we will be exploring visual and verbal imagery, the realm of the metaphoric mind. Actually we already speak this language in the folksy phrases we use every day. Most of them paint a vivid picture. Here are a few emotions and the highly graphic images used to describe them:

Sadness or depression	I have the blues; he's singing the blues; he's in the dumps; in the pits; feeling down; in a black hole
Feeling stuck	on a treadmill; blocked; hitting my head against a brick wall
Impatience	at my wit's end; at the end of my rope; the straw that broke the camel's back
Anger	in a purple rage; red with rage; red in the face; hot under the collar; hot and bothered; I'm boiling; she boiled over; he's a walking time bomb; she blew up; he blew off steam; he blew his stack (or top)
Envy	green with envy; bitten by the green-eyed monster
Fear	frozen with fear; scared stiff; I white-knuckled it; she was white as a sheet; she turned ashen; he turned white; her face turned pale; the color drained from his face; yellow; yellow-bellied; he caved in; weak-kneed

Desire	red hot; purple passion
Confusion	muddy; murky; foggy; torn
Anxiety	my stomach was tied up in knots; butterflies in my stomach

These are visual images, but they are also highly sensory and visceral. We feel them in our bodies the way we feel the hot rays of the sun or the chill of a dark cloudy day. Notice how prevalent color and texture are in these phrases. And observe how graphic the visual images are: boiling over, blowing his top, stomach tied up in knots. One could draw literal cartoons of these images. In fact, many of my clients have done just that: created a drawing or sculpture named with one of these phrases.

The expressive arts

Sometimes we find the right words and phrases to describe our feelings. But sometimes we don't. What causes us to be at a loss for words when trying to express our feelings? I believe there are several reasons:

- We don't know how we feel.
- We have mixed feelings and can't sort them out.
- We know how we feel but are afraid to voice it.
- We have emotions but no "feelings" vocabulary to express them.
- We have feelings that don't translate easily into words.

To express emotions, we have to feel them first. How do we know what we feel? And after we've felt our emotions, how can we *express* instead of suppress or repress them? One answer is: through the expressive arts. I define the expressive arts as the use of art, music, dance, drama, or writing as a means for revealing and expressing one's inner life of emotions, dreams, and desires. Those of us working in the field of expressive arts therapy work in an interdisciplinary way. It has been demonstrated that, when the arts are used intermodally (that is to say, in combination or alternating between one and another) they become a powerful vehicle for experiencing, identifying, and communicating one's true feelings. Many expressive arts therapists combine two or more forms: dance and storytelling, for instance, or music, poetry, and art.

It's very important that you understand the difference between expressive arts and art for exhibition, performance, or publication. In expressive arts, there is absolutely no expectation to perform. This is not Art with a capital A. We're not attempting to make art for the sake of art. We're not making art to be exhibited in a gallery, or creating dance, music, or drama to be performed, or writing in order to get published. Criticism, perfectionism, or preoccupation with technique has no place in the expressive arts, except perhaps to be exposed for what it is. Rather than being art for art's sake, it's art for the person's sake. It is the *process* that matters most. You will see this in many case studies and illustrations in this book. As you read about the unfolding of a painting, sculpture, dance, song, or written piece, you'll get the inside story on what the person felt while he or she created it and the feelings and insights that were revealed. In expressive arts, as long as the art product captures what the soul needs to express, the work has served its purpose.

In order for feelings to speak, the process must be safe and free of judgment and externally imposed standards of aesthetics, technique, or style. This is soul art. If we want to really listen to our inner self, to our own truth, we must set the Inner Critic aside for a while. When self-criticism and external standards are removed, the expressive arts allow our soul voice to flow through more readily. Why? Because it's difficult to deceive ourselves with these media. We simply don't know how to lie about our feelings when exploring through the arts. We do that with words all the time. We sweep our emotions under the rug of excuses and rationalizations.

To make it safe, let me suggest that you use caution in sharing this work with others. If the person is supportive, fine. If he or she is critical, beware. You don't need anyone putting you down or your art making. That goes for your journal work as well as explorations in other art forms such as music or movement.

The arts as process, not product

We are all accustomed to viewing the arts from the place of spectator or audience. Actually participating in the process of art making may seem quite threatening. The Inner Art Critic starts chattering immediately about how "You can't draw (or write or dance)" and "You have no talent." Or it will say "You don't have time for this, you have more important things to do." Some people who already play an instrument or sing for their own enjoyment may have fun with music but get cold feet at the idea of crossing over into art or writing. The same is true for some trained visual artists who may become paralyzed at the thought of singing or writing. If fear has you in its grip at the mere prospect of art making, then all I ask is that you stay with the process and see what happens. Give it a try. You will not be judged or critiqued. The only critic you will have to contend with is the one inside your own head. Those are the old beliefs and attitudes that stop you from listening to your heart's desire and to your true self. You will be given some guidelines for becoming aware of that critical voice and dealing with it.

Sometimes art happens

Occasionally my clients or students find some of their pieces quite satisfying to the eye. They actually display some of their art therapy work in their homes or offices. If this happens for you, that's fine. Consider it a by-product of your therapeutic experience. I say this because to truly benefit from these activities, you must drop any expectations of producing an aesthetically pleasing finished product. I also caution you about displaying this work where critical people will see it and start ripping it to shreds verbally. As mentioned earlier, you don't need that negative feedback, and it could just shut you down completely.

You might enjoy some particular medium so much that you want to take classes or workshops in that art form. Great! But please be clear about the difference. Expressive arts are for you alone. If you start performing you'll miss the whole point of this book. The perfect product—an art piece, dance, or musical composition—is not the goal here. What matters most is experiencing your feelings and gaining insights.

Two brains, two hands: right, left, write

A central tool you'll be using is Creative Journaling. The Creative Journal brings writing and art together, enabling you to let the verbal left brain know what the visual and emotional right brain is feeling and seeing. The feelings come out through art, music, and dance. However, deeper insights are often gained afterward while writing. The result is greater awareness of your feelings so that you can make more informed choices in your life. These techniques also help develop intuition, a right-brain function. Students report that the more they use their right hemisphere, the greater their access to intuitive information, such as hunches that help them in business, relationships, personal health, and more.

Some Creative Journal assignments go even further. They allow the hemispheres to communicate with each other. I'm referring to my method of written inner dialogues in which both hands alternate back and forth. You'll be using both your dominant and nondominant hands. I define the dominant hand as the one you normally write with. The nondominant is the other hand. My research shows that, right-handed or left-handed, writing and drawing with the nondominant hand give you greater access to the right-hemisphere functions: feelings, intuition, gut instinct, inner wisdom, and spirituality. Perhaps it is because the nondominant hand was never hardwired to the language centers of the brain. It has been left free to express nonverbal, nonrational perceptions. As you saw in my own case, this illiterate, unschooled hand also brings us to our emotional Inner Child. It is very common for people to feel childlike while printing with the nondominant hand, as I did in my early therapy sessions. Try it for yourself.

Get a pen and some paper and print your name using your nondominant hand. Then continue writing. Answer these questions:

- How does it feel to write with your nondominant hand?
- Is it awkward? Slow? Do you feel silly, stupid, childish, childlike?
- Is it fun? Relaxing? Creative? Liberating?
- Did you make mistakes in spelling and grammar?
- Did you judge yourself for poor penmanship?

Facing the critic

We all have a critical voice in our head that puts us down and constantly finds fault with us. It's called the Inner Critic. Chances are you heard it when you tried writing with your nondominant hand. It loves to find spelling errors and point out "bad penmanship," or tell us we're too slow or messy. This part of us learned what to say from the critics in our life: parents, siblings, teachers, bosses, spouses, etc. Let's take a look at what yours has to say and then have some fun answering back.

Answering back

With your dominant hand, write down what your Inner Critic says about your ability to engage in the kinds of expressive arts activities described so far. Don't think about it in advance or censor this voice in any way. Just keep the pen moving as fast as you can. When you're finished, read on.

Example:

CRITIC: What a joke! You think you're going to express yourself with art and writing and, did she say music? Who are you kidding? You couldn't draw your way out of a wet paper bag. And write! You're the worst writer that ever lived. You can't even draft a memo at the office without going to pieces. Come on. Get serious. You've got so much work to do. Look at that pile of stuff on your desk. You've got letters to write and mail that isn't even opened yet. Not to mention telephone calls to return. And then there's the laundry, and don't you think you should do some gardening today?

After the Inner Critic has had its say, switch the pen to your other hand, but don't write yet. First, read back what the Critic told you. Then get in touch with a feisty, assertive part of yourself. I call it the Inner Brat. If you've been a good boy or girl all your life, you may have to dig deep for this one. But it will be worth finding.

With your nondominant hand (the hand you don't normally write with) answer back to the Inner Critic by printing or writing, and really assert yourself. You don't have to be polite. You can even use four-letter words if you want.

Example:

ASSERTIVE SELF: You know what? I'm sick to death of this. I'm tired of being put down by you all the time and told what I'm capable of doing. All I hear from you is how I am *not* creative, how I make mistakes all the time. I can always count on you to throw a wet blanket over my dreams and true wishes. If you can't say anything helpful, then I want you to shut up. Make no mistake about it. I *am* going to do this.

The three brains

Going beyond right- and left-brain functions, there is another body of research that bears directly on emotional expression. It is the triune brain theory developed by Dr. Paul D. MacLean, formerly chief of the National Institute of Mental Health Laboratory for Brain Evolution. MacLean describes three separate but intimately connected brains, each nestled into the other. Each brain reflects a distinct stage of human evolution. The oldest, deepest region is called the reptilian brain. Corresponding to the medulla, pons, and spinal chord, it governs survival instincts, such as food finding, mating, defense, and habitual behavior. Above that is the next region called the old mammalian brain or the limbic system. It is the seat of emotions and also receives and processes input, which it communicates to the other two layers of the brain. The most recent, outermost layer is the new mammalian brain or neocortex. It has been described as the thinking cap, which controls abstract reasoning.

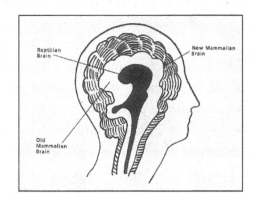

In addition to MacLean's work, there is some interesting brain research being done in Cleveland, Ohio, by neurosurgeon Dr. Robert White and a team at Case Western Reserve University. In conversations with Dr. White, he told me that image systems, such as SPECT scans, are being used to measure areas of the brain that are active when one feels strong emotions and even sexuality. Brain areas that are activated during spiritual experiences, such as prayer, meditation, and other kinds of religious experience, have been identified as well. Newberg and d'Aquili have published similar research at the University of Pennsylvania.

I was reminded of some other brain and soul research done by pioneering dream psychologist Alvaro Lopez-Watermann. Many years ago I was asked to supervise Alvaro's graduate degree studies, extensive dream research and interpretation techniques for finding guidance in dreams. Alvaro studied ancient spiritual traditions of India, such as Kashmir Shaivism, which teaches about the four states of consciousness. Alvaro drew on MacLean's triune brain theory, clinical work with his own clients, and insights received from dreams. Alvaro has suggested that there is a fourth part of the brain, which he calls the Peiskian brain. It is the pineal gland, which some Eastern spiritual traditions say is the seat of the soul and has a transcendental function. It appears to be the receptor that connects us to what some call divine or universal mind.

So what does all this have to do with emotions and insight into ourselves? Plenty. It seems that the limbic system is the part of the brain that harbors our emotions. However, it is often blocked off from conscious awareness. Recent research shows what Freud, Jung, and all the pioneers of psychotherapy knew: there is actually a gating mechanism that prevents us from remembering painful experiences. For survival, the feeling Inner Child goes into the closet and closes the door behind it. This was a necessary step in order to endure the challenges that life was presenting. I have even seen clients draw pictures or sculpt an image of this gating mechanism symbolically. It usually takes the form of a cave or closet sheltering a hurt and often mistrustful child who needs protection.

Sooner or later the feeling self must be taken out of the deep freeze if we are to be fully alive. Healing happens when we can contact what Hugh Missildine called the child of the past who is still very much alive in our emotions. There are no words to describe that magical moment when one literally draws these feelings out of hiding. What usually follows are deep insights and a sense of profound inner peace and well-being. Often a voice of inner wisdom comes through with spiritual guidance and strength. These flashes of inner truth or spiritual awareness are the same experiences that people who meditate and pray describe and that scientists are now measuring in laboratories. It was no surprise when Dr. White mentioned the possible connection between emotional and spiritual centers in the brain. I've observed it hundreds of times in therapy sessions while working with clients.

Expressive arts: matching the medium to the mood

How do we get from emotional expression to insight and spiritual wisdom? One way is through the expressive arts and the Creative Journal, including right- and left-hand dialogues, which connect both sides of the brain. For instance, in expressive arts, certain arts media seem to evoke a particular family of feelings. There are many reasons for this. The first is the nature of the medium itself and the kind of physical engagement it requires. For example, clay is a highly malleable substance that invites vigorous manipulation. It can be pounded, slapped, and twisted without being damaged. In fact, when potters prepare the clay for eventual firing in a kiln, that is exactly what they do to it. They call this wedging the clay. Any emotion that releases itself naturally through vigorous movements is a perfect match for clay. One ceramist I knew put it this way: "Working with clay is the best therapy I ever found. Clay can take whatever I have to dish out—frustrations, anger, impatience." Another medium that lends itself to vigorous movements and strong pressure is crayons on paper or cardboard. That's one reason why they use crayons with kids. The paper might tear, but the crayons themselves can withstand almost anything. Sure, they sometimes break, but the crayon pieces can still be used.

Some emotions evoke expression through body movement. Feelings of vulnerability might call one to assume a fetal position or wrap oneself in a blanket (real or imagined) for protection, warmth, and comfort. Feelings of joy may flow out easily through outstretched arms and a lively dance. Some emotions, like sadness or melancholy, might be rendered best in music or song. And then there are the emotions connected to different parts of our personality: the playful and Creative Child Within, the serene and wise part of us, the angry and rebellious Inner Brat, the enthusiastic adventurer, and many more. These lend themselves to mask making and dramatic dialogues, role-playing, and storytelling.

Learning the language of feelings is like learning any language. Experience comes first, then the language of the experience. The word *apple* would mean nothing if you'd never seen or eaten an apple. Emotional literacy is no different. Feeling comes first, verbal expression and insight follow.

In expressive arts the medium is the messenger of emotions. By interacting with the medium, feelings are evoked, but so are insights. We discover that our feelings carry profound inner wisdom. We find out what our feelings have to teach us.

As we learn about each art form, we will also see its appropriateness for specific feelings. In many cases I combine media, like drawing and music, or mask making and writing.

A general list of materials appears below. However, it is not necessary to get them all at once. You can't do all the activities in this book right away. It will take a few weeks or longer, depending on how much time you want to devote. The materials are listed according to the chapter where they are introduced. It's a good idea to read the chapter before you buy the materials for it. There are some alternatives that you can choose from, and you may even have some of these materials already.

Materials

All Chapters
Journal (8½" x 11"), blank hardbound book, or spiral sketch pad

Felt pens (twelve colors or more) with fine tip for writing

Felt markers (twelve colors or more) with wide tip for drawing

Chapter Three
Crayons or oil pastels (twelve colors or more)

Drawing paper, white (18" x 24" or approximately 12" x 18")

Chapter Four
Plain newsprint paper (18" x 24")

Chalk pastels

Spray fixative or hair spray (to prevent pastel drawings from smudging)

Box of watercolor paints and brushes (tubes or colors in pans)

Jar of water

Magazines with lots of photos and visual images

(Optional: colored paper, i.e., construction or origami paper)

Scissors

Glue

Paper towels

Trash container

Smock or old shirt or apron

Sound system for playing recorded music

Recorded music: your own or music recommended in the chapter, such as music for *The Mozart Effect, Volume III,* compiled by Don Campbell, or "Love" from Jessie Alan Cooper's *The Sound of Feelings*

Chapter Five

Red clay (Laguna air-drying red clay, EM 207, or comparable)

Work surface (wood, Masonite, or heavy cardboard)

Heavy piece of string for cutting clay

Bowl of warm water

Plastic airtight container for storing smaller pieces of clay

Chapter Six

Sound system for playing recorded music

Recorded music: your own or music recommended in the chapter

CD set: *The Sound of Feelings* by Jessie Allen Cooper

Art supplies

Chapter Seven

Sound system for playing recorded music

Recorded music: your own or music recommended in the chapter

Audiotape or CD: *Endless Wave, Volume I* by Gabrielle Roth

Audiotape or CD set: *The Sound of Feelings* by Jessie Allen Cooper

Art supplies

Chapter Eight

Drawing paper, white (18" x 24" or approximately 12" x 18")

Magazines

(Optional: colored paper, i.e., construction or origami paper)

Scissors

Glue

Chapter Nine

Art supplies

Tempera paint and brushes

Collage supplies

Mask-making supplies: plaster cloth strips (such as Activa brand) for making the mask form, Vaseline, old towels, paper towels, your choice of decorative elements such as ribbons, colored tissue paper, cellophane, yarn, fabric, cardboard

Large brown bags from supermarket for bag masks

Chapter Ten

Journal and felt pens

Art paper and collage materials

Embracing Your Creative Self

In order to more fully appreciate and enjoy the activities in this book, let me suggest that you tap into your Creative Self. Instead of describing it to you, I'd rather that you experience it firsthand for yourself.

With paper and pen, have a little conversation with your Creative Self. *Your* voice writes with the dominant hand. The Creative Self writes with the *nondominant hand.* Ask your Creative Self to tell you about itself: How has it already been active in your life? What role did it play in your accomplishments, hobbies, development of talents? How does it want to express itself in your life at this time? What does it want to explore with the techniques presented in this book?

3. FEELINGS IN YOUR BODY

Common sense tells us that feelings get stored in the body. Think about the body metaphors we use every day to describe emotional discomfort:

He gives me a pain in the neck.
I'm sick of shouldering all the responsibilities around here.
She got hot under the collar.
He blew his top.

This list could go on and on. We know instinctively what emotions these phrases bring to mind. Someone who *blows his top* is angry. We feel irritated or peeved at anyone we consider *a pain in the neck*. Without having to read a book or take a class we know that physical feelings and emotional feelings are deeply connected. In fact, many physical symptoms may be disguising unfelt emotions. Lurking under those annoying aches and pains, chronic conditions, or temporary discomforts, there may be a whole network of feelings desperately trying to be heard and released.

I have interviewed dozens of massage therapists, bodyworkers, and other health practitioners over the past thirty years on the subject of emotions in the body. Although they represented a broad range of techniques and types of training (such as Swedish massage, Rolfing, acupuncture, and movement therapy), they agreed on one thing. Body pain can be seen as a divining rod that leads us to stored emotions. Some practitioners refer to these buried feelings as cellular memories. Often when the patient is treated for a chronic or acute condition, emotions that have been denied or stuffed come pouring out of hiding. Digging up these emotions may be accompanied by a flashback to the time this particular emotion got stored. This may trigger tears or other strong expressions of emotion. For instance, deep tissue massage on a person's shoulder area may evoke memories of a time when he first began carrying other people's burdens—financial, emotional, or otherwise. Feelings of resentment and anger may erupt into awareness. Body-centered practitioners who work with emotions tell me that feelings stored in body parts get attention through localized pain messages or symptoms. When those areas are touched and worked on, the emotions get released from the prison of the body. After the emotions are expressed, frequently a great sense of relief follows. This often results in a decrease or complete disappearance of the physical pain or condition. After that, if the individual makes a conscious choice to start feeling emotions at the time they come up instead of stuffing them in the body, the results can be life changing. Mental and physical health can be transformed.

Emotions as energy

Emotions are energy. They are part of the human condition and part of our physical self. When they are in motion—e(nergy) + motion—feelings move in and through us.

They ebb and flow like the tides. Emotions are important for our physical survival. When crossing city streets we use caution born of fear—the fear of being hit by a car. As adults we listen to our queasy feelings when doing business with con men or opportunists. "Something doesn't feel right," we say to ourselves, and avoid being taken advantage of. Our emotions also take us to higher levels of human achievement. Anger about injustice and prejudice can be transformed into political activism emphasizing compassion for the victims. Grief over the death of a loved one or a public figure sometimes catalyzes action in a desire to "keep the person's spirit alive." Emotions move us—internally and also externally. They fire us up, motivate us, compel us into action. The person who cannot *feel* anything doesn't want to *do* anything, either. There is no joy, because there is no feeling. Lethargy sets in, and the body goes into a state of inertia. We describe people in this condition as having the lights on, but nobody's home. They're still living, but they are not *really* alive.

How emotions get stored in your body

When we judge certain emotions as unacceptable, we hide or squelch them in some way. If, as children, we were told "Big boys don't cry," or "It's not ladylike to be angry," or "Stop being a fraidy cat," then we started hiding the evidence of these taboo emotions. If our feelings are bad, then we must be bad for having them. First we conceal the feelings from others (suppression) and then we numb ourselves and try not to feel them anymore (repression). If it's not okay to express certain emotions, better to banish them altogether. To a child's mind, this makes sense. It may even be necessary for survival in a family that punishes kids for showing certain emotions, or rewards them for stuffing feelings.

Pamela is a perfect example. At age five, her parents divorced, moved away, and left her to live with her grandparents. She was told to be brave and not cry. In her youthful attempt to please her grandparents and hang on to the only security she had left, Pamela withheld her grief. It got stored in exactly the place where tears release: her sinuses. She suffered for thirty years with chronic allergies and sinus congestion. A string of medical specialists and many different medications had brought little relief, and she had almost given up hope. It was not until she was thirty-five years old and attending one of my journal classes that Pamela discovered her grieving child of the past. In a journal dialogue with her sinuses, the Inner Child popped out (through her nondominant hand) and scrawled, "I really want my mommy." Pamela sobbed for a long time, releasing years of unexpressed grief. Her Inner Child also said that it didn't like milk, indicating that she was allergic to it. After this dialogue, Pamela's sinus problems gradually vanished. If she ever felt the slightest symptom returning, she did one of these journal dialogues and always got relief by tuning in to her Inner Child's feelings.

Storing your feelings does not work. The energy of those emotions does not go away. Feelings will just hang around until we acknowledge them—and where they hang out is in the body. It's the only closet we have. So we may park all or some of our feelings there in storage lockers called body parts for years on end, but eventually they will burst out in the language of the body: physical sensations, aches, pains, low energy, and illness (either chronic or acute). Imagine a body with labels plastered all over it for emotions that have been stuffed inside. Most of us are walking around in that kind of body. In fact, try the following exercise and see for yourself.

FIND THE FEELING: YOUR BODY MAP

Materials
   Journal and felt pens
   Optional: Large white art paper and drawing materials, such as large felt pens, crayons, or oil or chalk pastels

Activity
   1. Using your *nondominant hand,* draw a simple outline of your body. Show both the front view and back. Don't worry about artistic skill. You're not being judged or cri-

tiqued here. Just make a silhouette as shown below. If you prefer, use the body charts in the Resources section.

2. Color in the areas of your body

   • where you usually carry tension or pain
   • where you are experiencing discomfort right now

Choose the colors that best represent the exact type of sensations you feel in that part of your body. For instance, if you feel hot in an area, you might want to use a warm color like red or orange. If you feel cold or numb, use colors that represent that for you. There is no right or wrong way to do this. Whatever colors you choose will be appropriate. You can also represent the sensations with the type of strokes you use. Sharp pains might show as jagged lines. Heaviness might be depicted with a solid mass of color. Explore and experiment.

3. With your *nondominant hand,* write an emotion word on or next to each area that was colored in on your body outline.

4. With your *dominant hand,* jot down in your journal any observations you made about your picture.

Reclaiming our emotions

The picture you have drawn may show many colored-in areas. This is a clear sign that you are carrying around lots of stored emotions in your body. This discovery will now allow you to get these painful emotions out of your body. Whether the person had one pain or many, I have seen amazing transformations in my workshops and private practice through the use of drawing, writing, and other expressive arts. Turning suppression and repression into creative expression holds the key. And it's as close as your fingertips.

People tend to store their unwanted emotions in different parts of the body. For one, it may be the shoulders, and for another, the head. Still another person might carry emotions in the lower back. You've probably located familiar trouble spots easily when you colored in your body map. A classic case of someone who healed her body and emotions through written expression was one of my early students, Lucille. An attractive wife and mother in her fifties, she had been plagued with chronic cystitis (bladder infections) for about thirty years. Her physician had become so concerned that he advised her to undergo exploratory surgery. At the time, Lucille was taking one of my Creative Journal classes where I had just taught the group how to actually draw and dialogue with their bodies. When confronted with the specter of hospitalization, Lucille quite courageously told her doctor about this and said she wanted to have a little talk with her bladder before being admitted. There was a dead silence, followed by: "Well, okay, Lucille. But if the symptoms are still there on Monday, you're going into the hospital." She agreed.

When she sat down and had a journal chat with her bladder, the following is what came out. I've emphasized certain words that have, as you will see, both physical and emotional implications.

Bladder: I am your bladder and I don't like the way you are holding back on me. You're not being honest with me.

Lucille: Well, I'm angry.

Bladder: So you're angry. Why don't you tell me what you're angry about?

Lucille: Because I'm just one ball of fury and it's very frightening to me to be so angry.

Bladder: Well, it doesn't help me any for you to fill me up with your anger. If you'd just let some of it out at the time you feel it, instead of holding it in, then the poison wouldn't all back up in me.

Lucille: I'm not sure you'd love me if you knew how angry I was.

Bladder: Love you, why I'd be able to love you more. It's your anger that keeps us apart.

Lucille: But I need that anger because I'm afraid of being too close.

Bladder: What would it mean to you if we did get too close?

Lucille: Then you'd get to know all about me. Especially the rotten part.

Bladder: I don't know of any rotten part.

Lucille: I know you don't, but I do and I have to live with it every day of my life.

Bladder: You mean the part that failed to succeed?

Lucille: Why, yes, how did you know?

Bladder: Why, I've known all the time, but that doesn't make me love you less.

Lucille: Do you really mean that?

Bladder: Of course I do. I have succeeded to fail and you failed to succeed. I really don't understand success and failure anyway.

Lucille: I guess I don't either. That sure makes me feel better. There is much too much energy spent on success and failure. I guess I've been too intense about it. It's a good feeling not to have to be concerned or worry whether I'm succeeding or failing all the time. It kind of reminds me of school and being concerned about my grades and whether I passed or failed that particular class.

Bladder: Yeah. *The pressure was terrible.* I'm glad we don't get grades on our knowledge or performance today.

Lucille: Geez, can you believe the pressure we put on ourselves today when we don't have to.

Bladder: I'm glad we had this talk because I sure feel a lot better. Thanks.
                                    —*The Creative Journal: The Art of Finding Yourself*

Fear of anger, dread of judgment, pressure on yourself to succeed: these are all familiar themes in psychotherapy and counseling. Yet they play themselves out in very unique and original ways in each person. In Lucille's case, these issues were reflected in the very tissues of her bladder. The common term *pissed off* comes to mind as a literal description of her particular form of anger. Anger that was held in because she was afraid to let anyone see it. Somewhere along the line she'd been taught that anger was unladylike, not acceptable. Referring to her held-in anger, the bladder wants her to let it out when she feels it. Yet her bladder might as well be talking about urine. Anyone who has been plagued with bladder infections knows that one contributing factor can be postponing urination. Holding it in causes the poison to back up into the system, as Lucille's bladder says. Sufferers of cystitis also know about the constant feeling of *pressure* in this area, another theme that occurs in Lucille's dialogue.

At one point Lucille writes, "It's very frightening to me to be so angry." She is afraid of showing her "rotten part" or, more precisely, the parts of herself that she judges as rotten. So she stores it all in her body as anger, fear of anger, anger at her fear.

On the other hand, Lucille's bladder is all-forgiving. It does not judge her or in-dulge in name-calling—even though she used to call it names, saying, "I have a bad bladder." The bladder even says, "I failed to succeed," referring to her long history of doctors' visits and medication for this troublesome condition. But it goes on to ques-tion the very concept of success and failure, and of judgment. Underneath her chronic bladder problems are a network of intertwined judgments, emotions, and negative self-talk (*Anger is not okay. I've got rotten parts that I can't let anyone see. They won't love me if I'm angry. I'm a failure*). Underneath these judgments, we see feelings of fear, anger, and being pressured, festering away.

By the dialogue's end we see that the bladder plays the role of patient (the part that is sick) as well as the diagnostician (telling the emotional cause). It is also the healer, offering Lucille sound advice along with unconditional love. The body did talk. And it had a lot to say. It is obvious that a voice of deep inner wisdom and unconditional love was waiting to be heard.

Following this conversation with her bladder, Lucille's symptoms cleared up com-pletely. She did not require exploratory surgery nor did this long-standing condition recur. I stayed in touch with Lucille for many years afterward and was gratified to learn that she had followed her talent for writing and had created many autobiographical pieces about her life. She was even featured in a film about older women entitled *Act-ing Our Age,* and I attended the premiere with her. Lucille created a new life at a time when most people are retiring.

Incidentally, according to the ancient art of Chinese medicine (which includes acupuncture and herbal medicine), the organs are paired up, and there is a specific emotion associated with each pair. Too much or too little of that emotion can put those particular organs out of balance.

Kidney/bladder = fear
    Think of a child who is frightened and wets his pants.
Liver/gall bladder = anger
    Someone who "has a lot of gall" is seen as pushy and aggressive.
Heart/small intestine = joy
    A "broken heart" comes from absence of joy.
Spleen/pancreas = sympathy/worry
    Imbalance here can be associated with worrying too much about
    others as well as oneself.
Lung/large intestine = grief
    Pamela's Inner Child described her bronchial tubes as hurting be-
    fore she cried out her grief.

Like Lucille and Pamela, many of my students and clients have done body dia-logues and uncovered emotions in certain organs that correlate perfectly with the Chi-nese system. None of them had ever read about or studied acupuncture or been treated by a practitioner of Chinese medicine. There is an ancient wisdom that we contact in these dialogues that knows far more than the rational mind does. That wisdom is read-ily accessible through drawing and dialoguing with the nondominant hand. You'll be engaging in the kind of dialogues Lucille and Pamela were engaged in, in order to find your own feelings—both physical and emotional—and discover the voice of wisdom and healing within yourself. Before we do that, let's learn to become more sensitive to the language of the body.

Feeling the body

When clients or students tell me they have a hard time finding their feelings, I often direct them back home to their bodies. A good place to look for emotions is in the parts of our bodies that are speaking up. Since the body speaks in the language of physical sensations, we need to start there. Later on we can translate those sensations into colors, shapes, textures, sounds, and then into words that describe emotions.

Let's begin with a body meditation. Read through the guidelines and then close your eyes during steps 1–3.

WHAT YOU SEE IS WHAT YOU FEEL

Materials
  Journal and felt pens
  Optional: Large white art paper and drawing materials, such as large felt pens, crayons, or oil or chalk pastels.

Activity
  1. Get into a comfortable seated position or lie down on your back on the floor. If seated in a chair, make sure your feet are flat on the floor. Take everything off your lap. If lying down, have your feet about a foot apart.
  2. Close your eyes and place your hands on your belly, just below your navel. Allow yourself to breathe in and out and become aware of your breathing. Allow the breath to go down into your belly and feel that area rising on the inhale and contracting on the exhale. Allow the breathing to be deep and slow and rhythmic.
  3. Take a sensory awareness trip through your body. Starting at the top of your head, feel all the sensations there. Then slowly move down your face from forehead

to chin and jawline, checking out the sensations inside your eyes and mouth and throat as well. Then tune in to your ears and back of your head. Continue down your neck both front and back, shoulders, arms, palms, and fingers (one side, then the other).

Check out the sensations inside your torso: chest, heart and lungs, upper back. Then move your awareness down to your midsection: stomach, liver and gall bladder area, spleen, pancreas, and the kidneys in the back. It doesn't matter whether or not you know where these organs are, just feel whatever sensations are going on in this part of your body.

A very bright and hardworking college student was plagued with test anxiety. She drew how her body felt when she was gripped with fear before an exam. Her *stomach was tied up in knots*. After doing this drawing, the condition vanished and she was able to relax and sit for exams with confidence.

Next, move your awareness to your pelvic area: intestines, bladder, reproductive system and genitals, and your anus and buttocks. Then complete the journey through your body by becoming aware of each leg: hip, thigh, knee, calf and shin, ankle, top and sole of the foot, and each toe.

4. Draw an outline of your body or use a photocopy of the appropriate body chart at the back of the book. Color in all the parts of your body that are sending out strong signals at this time: pain, discomfort, achiness, or pleasure and relaxation. Choose the colors and make the strokes that best represent each sensation. Have fun exploring and experimenting.

5. Select one body part that is talking the loudest: the strongest pain, the most discomfort. On a separate sheet of paper, draw a picture of that body part, showing the
nature of the pain or discomfort you feel there. Don't worry about the artistic merit
of your drawing. Simply let yourself picture it the way you feel it. Choose the colors that best represent the sensations you feel in that part of your body.

Locating physical discomfort caused by stored emotions can become a regular meditation practice. It is a great relaxation technique as well as a way to access emotions
you are having trouble identifying. Color in the feelings first, name them later. Sometimes students feel physically and emotionally better after just doing this part of the
exercise, but there is more. As you saw, it is possible to interpret your own physical sensations (and body drawings) with words. That is what you'll be doing next.

What the drawing means

Interpreting pattern and color in your drawings is really quite simple. It doesn't require
any special talent or training in symbolism, and you don't need a degree in psychology
or art therapy. It's your drawing and those are your symbols. They are personal and
unique to you. Instead of trying to analyze the picture, students of my work have discovered that a far more direct and truthful route is through the dialogue form you saw
in Lucille's case study.

The body as storyteller

In this step of the treasure hunt to find your real feelings, you'll be consulting with
your body, asking it some simple questions and getting some profound insights.

FEEL ME, HEAL ME

Materials

Journal and felt pens

Optional: Large white art paper and drawing materials, such as large felt pens, crayons, or oil or chalk pastels

Activity

1. Draw a new picture of the body part that is speaking the loudest through pain and discomfort.

2. In your journal, have a written conversation with the body part. Use two contrasting colors. With your *dominant hand,* ask the following questions:

   - Who or what are you?
   - How do you feel?
   - What is causing you to feel this way?
   - What can I do to help you?
   - What are you here to teach or tell me?

   With your *nondominant hand,* answer the questions. This is very important. Answers from the *nondominant hand* and right brain are usually more expressive of bodily sensations and emotions. They also tap directly into a state of intuitive wisdom and guidance associated with the right brain.

3. When your dialogue is complete, imagine what it would be like if these feelings were no longer stuffed in your body and didn't need to speak to you through physical pain. What would your body feel like? With your *nondominant hand,* draw a picture of your whole body feeling relaxed, energized, and healthy. Around the picture, let the body you have portrayed write about how it feels in the first-person present tense. Use your *nondominant hand.* If, after doing step 2 above, you already

feel relief from your symptoms, then simply draw your body as it feels now and describe it in writing.

Journal your reflections on this chapter. Review what you learned and what insights came out of the journaling you did with the above exercises. Write about it using your dominant hand.

Note: If you'd like a recorded narration for the body journey, use my CD *The Picture of Health: Meditation and Writing/Drawing Exercise* (see Resources: Books, audio and video cassettes). To explore more fully the wisdom of the body and hear some other case histories, listen to my audiotape series *The Wisdom of Your Other Hand* (Sounds True Audio). In this set of five tapes, there is one titled *The Body as Storyteller* and another on *The Inner Family* that includes discussion of how body parts carry our emotions, our Inner Child, and more.

PART TWO

Expressing Your Feelings

The ABCs of feelings:
match the medium to the mood

You will now embark on the adventure of exploring feelings through the expressive arts: drawing, painting, collage, sculpting, music and sound, movement and dance, writing, dramatic dialoguing, and more. You'll be matching your feelings with the medium that is most likely to evoke and illuminate that particular emotion. This is not meant to limit you by any means. You can express any emotion with any medium you like. It is rather a set of suggestions, for some media tend to draw out certain feelings more directly than others. For example, if you want to express anger a crayon allows you to press hard, exert lots of fiery energy, and use strong color. By comparison, soft chalk pastels in subtle colors aren't as well suited for expressions of anger. They crumble under pressure and don't hold up well with strong strokes. Watercolors in paint pans are often subtle in hue when mixed with water (unless you use the kind that comes in tubes), and painting with small brushes doesn't evoke the kind of large or forceful gesture that anger usually requires. On the other hand, clay can be pounded and punched and is therefore a great medium for releasing rage, resentment, or frustration.

Remember, this is *process* art. The way you work with the medium and the experience you have with it are more important than the finished product. I can't emphasize that enough. If you get all hung up on the end product, then you'll miss the whole point of expressive arts. This is about *you and your feelings,* not about Art with a capital A. This is about allowing emotions—all of them—to come out through the creative vent. If some of your expressive art slips over into aesthetically compelling pieces that you want to develop further, great! But that is definitely not the goal. Likewise, if buried talents surface and you want to cultivate them, you have my full encouragement, but performance-oriented activities belong in another arena.

Since this is a guidebook to be used again and again depending on which feelings are coming up at the time, I have included here a Directory of Emotions in alphabetical order. Some of these feeling words are accompanied by page numbers referring to activities that relate directly to that emotion. After you've gone through this book and done the activities, this directory can point you to an activity that is suited for the feeling of the moment.

This directory is also useful for developing a feelings vocabulary that you can use in everyday life. The more you practice naming your emotions, the easier it will be to express them directly to others instead of stuffing them inside.

Anytime you want, you can turn to this directory for activities and ideas on how to release and accept a particular emotion. Some days you may come to this book already knowing how you feel. At other times you might need to identify your particular emotion through the exercises in Part I. Or you may find the precise word for your feeling in the directory. The directory is intended to help you locate an activity that can get you started.

Once you begin, you may branch out into other feelings and activities. As you've seen in previous examples, you may start with one emotion then find that there are several others hidden below that. Anger may surface first only to reveal hurt or grief buried underneath.

Many feelings in the directory are closely linked to each other. If there is no page number next to the word that matches your mood, read on until you find one that is close. For example, feeling *abandoned* is often associated with such emotions as sadness, loneliness, helplessness, isolation, etc. In other words, these emotions travel in groups or families. Being precise about finding the word that really describes your particular feeling is an important exercise in developing emotional literacy. Starting with an activity that evokes a whole family of emotions, like sadness, can help you express a specific feeling more fully, such as grief over the death of a loved one.

Directory of emotions
an alphabetical reference guide to emotions

Abandoned
Adequate
Admiration
Adoring
Adventurous
Affectionate
Afraid: 95–97, 128

Agitated
Alone
Amazed
Ambivalent: 89–94
Amused
Angry: 81–89, 116–20,
    141, 169–70
Annoyed
Antagonistic
Anxious
Appreciative
Aroused
Ashamed

Assertive: 169
Astounded
Attracted
Awed

Bashful
Belonging
Bewildered
Bitter
Blessed
Blissful
Bold
Brave

Burdened

Burned out

Calm

Captivated

Cautious

Chagrined

Challenged

Cheerful

Cheerless

Childlike

Combative

Compassionate

Concerned

Confident

Conflicted

Confused: 89–95

Contented: 103–5, 145,
    148–50, 171

Contrite

Courageous

Creative: 101–2, 105–7,
    171–72

Crushed

Defeated

Dejected

Delighted

Depressed: 97–98, 128,
    146, 166–67

Deserving

Desirous

Despairing

Desperate

Despondent

Devoted

Determined

Diffident

Disappointed

Disconnected

Discontented

Discouraged

Disgruntled

Disgusted

Disheartened

Dispirited

Distraught

Distressed

Disturbed

Divided

Down

Drained

Dread

Eager

Ecstatic

Electrified

Embarrassed

Empathic

Empty

Encouraged

Enjoyment

Enthusiastic

Envious

Estranged

Euphoric

Exasperated

Excited

Fascinated

Fearful: 95–97, 128,
    166–67

Flustered

Forlorn

Fragmented: 89–94

Frantic

Free

Friendly

Frightened

Frustrated

Fulfilled

Furious

Gay

Giddy

Glad

Gleeful

Gloomy

Glum

Grateful

Gratified
Grieving: 97–101, 127–28,
    145–46, 166–67
Guilty

Happy: 101–2, 107–8,
    150–51, 168–69,
    171–72, 218
Hateful
Helpful
Helpless: 99–101
Hesitant
Homesick
Hopeful
Hopeless
Horrified
Hostile
Humble
Hurt
Hysterical

Impatient
Indecisive
Indignant
Infatuated
Infuriated
Insecure
Inspired
Invigorated

Jealous
Joyful: 101–2, 105–7,
    171–72, 187,
    205–6
Joyous

Kind

Lazy
Lighthearted
Listless
Lonely: 97–101, 127–28,
    145–46, 166–67
Longing
Lost
Loving: 101–2, 107–8,
    150–51, 168–69,
    215–17
Lovestruck
Low

Mad: 81–84, 116–20,
    141, 169–70
Manic
Melancholic: 97–101
Mischievous
Miserable
Moody
Mournful

Naughty
Nervous: 95–97
Numb
Nurtured
Nurturing: 168–69,
    215–17

Optimistic
Outraged
Overjoyed
Overwhelmed

Pained
Pampered
Panicked or panicky
Passionate
Peaceful: 103–5, 148–50,
    170–71, 177–78
Perplexed
Petrified
Pleased
Playful: 101–2, 105–7,
    171–72, 205–6
Powerful
Powerless
Pressured
Protective: 169
Proud
Put off

Quiet

Rageful: 81–89, 116–20,
    141, 169–70
Rapturous
Rebellious
Regretful
Relaxed
Relieved
Remorseful
Renewed
Repelled
Repulsed
Resentful: 81–89
Respectful
Restless
Reverent
Revolted

Sad: 97–98, 127–28,
    145–46, 166–67
Safe
Satisfied
Scared: 95–97, 128,
    166–67
Scattered: 89–95
Scornful
Secure
Self-confident
Self-conscious

Self-pitying
Serene: 103–5, 148–50,
    170–71, 177–78
Settled
Shaky
Sheepish
Shocked
Shy
Silly
Solemn
Sorrowful
Sorry
Spiteful
Stressed
Stuck
Stunned
Stupefied
Suffering
Surprised
Suspicious
Sympathetic

Tenacious
Tender
Tentative
Terrified
Threatened
Thrilled
Thwarted
Timid

Torn: 89–94
Tranquil
Trapped
Troubled
Trusting

Uncomfortable
Uneasy
Unsafe
Unsettled
Unsure
Uptight

Vexed
Violated
Violent
Vulnerable: 99–101,
    128, 146, 166–67

Warm
Wary
Weak
Weary
Weepy
Whimsical
Withdrawn
Wonderment
Wrathful

Zany

4. THE COLOR OF EMOTIONS: FROM RED WITH RAGE TO FEELING BLUE

We already use visual images to convey emotions, so why not take the next step? This chapter will help you express feelings on paper through color, line, texture, shape, and image making. This medium works whether you have talent or experience in art or not. It works even if you do not know how you feel, for visual art is a wonderful way to both discover and express feelings. It is one of the ways our brain's right hemisphere speaks its mind. Visual art making is a passport to the realm of emotions, intuition, imagination, and creative breakthroughs. So be ready for some wonderful surprises and deep insights with help from parts of your brain that you may never have used before. Be willing to literally see into your very own heart and soul.

Materials you'll need

Journal (with unlined white paper)

Felt pens (fine and wide tip in assorted colors)

Art paper, white (18" x 24") drawing paper

Optional: colored art paper (12" x 18") for drawing and painting, such as Strathmore colored art paper pads, 300 series

Colored paper (such as construction paper, origami paper, etc.)

Crayons or oil pastels

Chalk pastels

Box of watercolors and brush (cake colors in paint pans or watercolors in tubes with palette)

Jar of water (for washing brushes)

Scissors

Glue (white glue, glue stick, or roll-on glue)

Old magazines with lots of photographs, such as *National Geographic, O, Vogue*

The ABCs of drawing: color, line, shape, and texture

As we saw from the common phrases above, color conveys quite accurately the characteristics of certain emotions. Feelings have energy and so do colors. Some emotions feel hot (like a red or orange sun), some are cool (like a blue lake), while others are dark (like a black night). You need no training to use color for expressing emotions. Just trust your instinct. Whatever color you choose is the right one for you at this time. We start by drawing emotions using simple abstract scribbles in color. In addition to color, drawing includes the other basic elements of visual art as well: line, shape, and texture. These are the building blocks we use as we explore feelings with visual arts. We'll also paint with watercolors and make collages.

The materials are simple to use. You'll probably remember them from kindergarten or even preschool. If your Inner Art Critic is starting to intrude with comments like "You don't know how to draw, you don't have any talent. This is kid stuff, you have more important things to do," just suggest that he or she take a coffee break while you read on and do the activities.

Drawing out your feelings

This first activity involves scribbling. If it makes you feel like a little kid, then give yourself a pat on the back because that's the whole idea. When you were a child you still felt your emotions—you hadn't succeeded in burying them yet. You didn't have words for your emotions, but you did *feel.* And you could frown, cry, hit, scream, giggle, laugh, and much more. There's no better place to find feelings than in the little child who is still alive inside.

THE FEELINGS TEST

Materials

Large white art paper or plain newsprint and drawing materials, such as felt pens, crayons, or oil pastels; journal

Activity

1. On the large art paper, using the drawing tool with your *nondominant hand,* make a scribble expressing each of the emotions listed below. Use the color that best describes each feeling. This is a very personal choice. There is no right or wrong way to do it. Follow your instincts. Use a different section of the paper for each scribble and use more than one sheet if necessary. Write the name of each emotion next to or under each scribble right after you've done it.

Note: You can also do this activity in your journal. If you do, use a different page for each scribble.

afraid

happy

angry

loving

frustrated

excited

sad

playful

depressed

silly

lonely

confident

confused

hopeful

peaceful

2. In your journal, with your *dominant hand,* answer the following:

   • Were any of these feelings difficult for you to express? If so, in what way were they difficult?
   • Did you have fun drawing any of these feelings? Which ones?

3. With your *dominant hand,* write about what it was like to draw the feeling that was most fun for you.

4. Continue writing with your *dominant hand,* but this time focus on the feeling you had the least fun drawing.

5. Which emotions from this list do you hide, and which ones do you express in your everyday life?

Make two lists with your *dominant hand:*

- Feelings I express
- Feelings I hide

6. Write any observations about yourself and any feelings that stand out. Use whichever hand you wish.

Perplexed

SCRIBBLE A FEELING

Materials

Large white art paper or plain newsprint and drawing materials, such as felt pens, crayons, or oil pastels; journal

Activity

1. Think about the last time you had a really strong emotion. (If you are experiencing one right now, work with that.) Using the large art paper, draw a picture of the emotion, with the drawing tool in your *nondominant hand.*

- What colors convey the emotion?
- What shape is it?
- What kinds of lines and textures best capture this emotion?

2. With your *nondominant hand,* write the name of the emotion somewhere on your picture. Then write a title for the drawing.

    Remember, there is no right or wrong way to do this. Listen to your instincts.

3. Look at your drawing. In your journal, write any observations with your *dominant hand.*

    - Was the feeling difficult for you to express?
    - Did you feel the emotion while you were drawing it?
    - Is it connected to any situation in your life right now? If so, write about it.

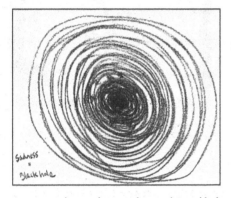

A woman drew sadness and named it a *black hole.* These feelings were linked with her watching her mother's health decline. After doing the drawing and talking about it, this young woman did another one.

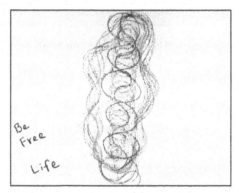

While doing her second drawing, a multicolored picture titled *Life,* the woman's spirits lifted dramatically. She expressed a resolve to find more time to play. It's as if she were saying: Life is precious; live it while you can.

Emotions at the boiling point: anger and rage

Emotions are like people: They simply do not want to be ignored, neglected, or ostracized. They will bang on the door until we let them in to join the family of other emotions that are part of our human condition. So let's open the door to anger, say hello, and welcome it inside. If we do, it's not going to hurt us or anyone else. It just wants to be recognized.

Volumes could be written about how anger that's held in over time contributes to stress and illness. Hate and resentment, for instance, have been found to release stress-producing hormones into the blood, accompanied by a weakening of the immune system for a full day. This is the stress response at work. Just as a chronic case of stuffed anger that has festered into resentment and hate can implode and damage our own health, it can also explode and hurt others. Stockpiling this powerful family of feelings can produce ammunition for uncontrollable and even violent outbursts.

A more productive way to deal with anger (and all its cousins) is to feel it, express it safely, and then use it creatively. Anger can save lives when it propels us to right action, or it can end lives when it erupts destructively. Anger can build our self-esteem, as in the case of the abuse survivor who turns rage into healthy assertiveness. Or it can tear us down, when we accept unfair treatment and turn our anger inward in the form of self-judgment, resentment, depression, or helplessness.

Let's begin with expressing and accepting the fact that we do indeed feel angry sometimes. Acceptance of anger is the key here, because our problems with this hot emotion stem from our unwillingness to admit we feel it. "Mad? Who me? I'm not mad. Whatever gave you that idea?" we bark when questioned on the subject, our tone of voice belying the truth. If we were taught that anger wasn't an okay emotion, we'll deny it at every turn. And therein lies the dilemma: the denial of this very real and human feeling.

One of the most public and visible ways that anger is expressed in our society is through graffiti. The four-letter words, phrases, and images that deface public walls and buildings shock and dismay us. We want to stamp it out. Yet what about the kids who are doing it? It has always been my belief that taggers are trying to tell us something in the only way they know how. If we'd provide open art studies for youngsters to vent their feelings on paper, canvas, and murals, I believe we'd see far less destruction of this type. In some areas kids have turned graffiti into an art form, and in a few cities, like Los Angeles and Santa Fe, community mural projects have given youngsters

CAUTION: **If you are a survivor of abuse and it is too terrifying for you to face your anger alone, then you will need professional help, if you are not already getting it. In attempting any of these activities, if emotions start to feel overwhelming for you, stop. I strongly recommend getting help. A good therapist can coach you through the fear and eventually make it safe for you to do these activities.**

Scribble Your Anger

Repeat the "scribble a feeling" activity above, but focus only on anger, rage, resentment, or some similar feeling. If you aren't feeling this way right now, go back to a recent time when you did feel such an emotion. On the other hand, if you are feeling angry about some situation in your life, let the emotion come out onto the page.

a creative visual voice. Emotions will come out, either creatively or destructively. It's up to us to choose.

Personal graffiti can be a wonderful way to let off steam at the time it's building up. One woman did this at work. Her boss, a real control freak, was giving everyone a hard time, and she was boiling over. If she had followed her impulses she probably would have gotten fired or quit. By going into the restroom and journaling page after page of angry graffiti, she was able to tell him off and feel temporarily satisfied without jeopardizing her job. She took charge of her feelings and dumped them instead of losing control of them and herself. She *had* her feelings instead of letting her feelings *have* her. Back at her desk, she could then get on with her work. This woman did resign a short while afterward, but not in a fit of rage. She waited until she had another job lined up and a good recommendation from her boss. In other words, she took good care of herself.

This next activity is a great way to release anger through words—even four-letter words—and simple images. We've all got a rebellious, angry brat inside. Isn't it time to let that side out in a productive way? You can use old newspapers or newsprint, or you can turn to the privacy of your journal if that feels more comfortable. I invite you to pull out all the stops and let it all hang out through your own personal graffiti.

GETTING IT OFF YOUR CHEST

Materials

Large white art paper or old newspaper, journal, large felt pens, crayons or oil pastels

Activity

1. With your *nondominant hand,* express your anger on the art paper (or in your journal) by creating graffiti. Use whatever words, phrases, or messages are necessary to convey this emotion. Don't think about it, just keep your hand moving.
2. Sit quietly afterward and see how you feel now. Do you feel like writing your observations about the activity? If so, write with your *dominant hand.*

The image of feelings

Earlier I listed some common images used to describe emotions. Now you're going to translate this kind of metaphoric right-brain thinking into your own portrayal of anger. This can be done with any feeling, but since we're focusing on anger-related emotions, that is the feeling I'd like you to draw. Again, color is an important component and so are the qualities of line, shape, and texture.

If your Inner Critic starts telling you again what you can't do, let me assure you that none of this matters. I'm not asking you to make Art. No one will criticize your draw-ing. You may not consider yourself a skilled artist, but you are learning to use a new language. It is understandable that you would feel clumsy and awkward at first. Even artists have a hard time with expressive arts because they're used to making art that looks good or can be exhibited or sold. I know, because that's where I was when I first discovered the power of expressive arts. As a professional with a degree in fine arts and lots of experience, I was horrified at my first attempts to draw out my real feelings. It looked ugly and primitive to me or rather to my Inner Art Critic. I thought I was los-ing it for sure. Fortunately, I hung in there and continued. I hope you will do the same, whether or not you're a trained and experienced artist.

PORTRAIT OF A FEELING, PART I

Materials

Large white art paper; drawing materials, such as felt pens, crayons, or oil pastels; journal. Optional: Colored art paper or construction paper instead of white paper

Activity

1. Reflect on the emotion of anger. Use any word you like: mad, pissed off, etc. Where do you feel it in your body? What is the sensation like? How does your whole body feel when you are angry?
2. With the drawing tool in your *nondominant hand*, draw a portrait of anger. (See ex-ample below.)
3. Sit quietly afterward and see how you feel now. Write any observations about your portrait of anger in your journal using your *dominant hand*.

    • Look at the colors you've used. What do they say about your feelings?
    • How about the lines? Are they heavy or light? Jagged and sharp?
    • Did you use textures that express anger? In what way?

Sometimes it can help to draw a more in-depth self-portrait of yourself in the grip of a particular emotion. This may take a little more time but can be just as cathartic as a quick scribble or graffiti session. Interpreting your drawings in your journal can bring deep insights into what makes you tick emotionally. One woman drew a very dramatic self-portrait of anger. It was done long before the research on how hate and resentment affect our bodies.

Our right-brain intuition just naturally knows how to create images that tell the truth about what's going on inside of us, both physically and emotionally. Drawing ourselves is like looking into a very special mirror. The difference is that art shows us our inner life, something that mirrors can never reflect back to us. Drawings also reveal more about how certain emotions affect specific parts of the body.

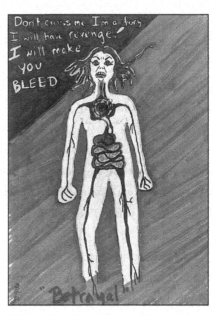

This is almost like an X ray of what was going on inside her body. By depicting her emotions graphically, this woman released a great deal of physical tension along with her anger. More important, she was able to see what the fury was doing to her body.

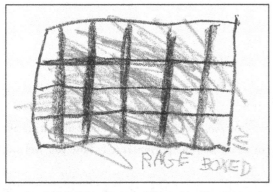

A red scribble inside a black cage shows that this woman tries to imprison her anger (stuff it), but it still spills out.

PORTRAIT OF A FEELING, PART 2

Materials

Same as above

Activity

1. With your *nondominant hand,* draw a picture of yourself feeling and expressing anger. Include any words or phrases that convey this emotion.
2. Sit with your finished drawing and tune in to your body and your emotions. How do you feel now physically? Emotionally?

As feelings of anger come to the surface, you might become aware of certain people you are angry at. If that is the case, you can use the following activity to vent your emotions in a safe place, your journal. Through writing, you can get these feelings out without confronting the other person. Just acknowledge the full strength of your feelings and express them. This is not about editing your remarks, nor is it anything you would show the other person. Rather, it is a way to dump your emotions out as you did with scribbling and graffiti. You are taking responsibility for your feelings.

DUMPING FEELINGS

Materials

Journal and felt pens

Activity

1. In your journal, with your *nondominant hand,* write a letter to someone you are angry at. It can be someone living or dead. Tell the person exactly how you feel and why you are angry.
2. In your journal, tell his person how you want to resolve the situation for yourself. Write this part with your *dominant hand.* This letter is for your eyes only.

The art of collage

One of the best two-dimensional media for releasing the hot feelings of anger and frustration is collage. Tearing paper or even fabric can be extremely satisfying when you're

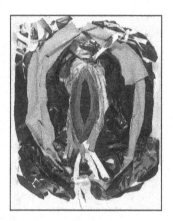

boiling over with any of these explosive feelings. The simple act of ripping things apart can be therapeutic in itself. One teenager told me that when she got really angry, she just went and tore up old out-of-date telephone directories. The sound of the paper ripping and the physical action of shredding the pages allowed her a much-needed release for emotions that bubbled up inside her and threatened to go out of control. Another medium that provides this release is clay, which will be explored in the next chapter. Anger and other feelings can also be released through sports and in dance, another art form we

will use later. Anything that allows us to physically release these emotions in a safe, nondestructive way is valuable.

Collage afforded me one of the most powerful and satisfying experiences I ever had using expressive arts. I had gotten word, indirectly, that one of my books had gone out of print. For an author, this is like having someone

stick a knife in your guts. All that work up in smoke! Even worse, I found out about it through the order department that was charged with remaindering the book. My editor didn't even have the decency to call me and let me know what was happening. I was shocked, hurt, disappointed, and furious at the shabby treatment I'd received! As they say, I saw red. See the collage and graffiti on this page and the next.

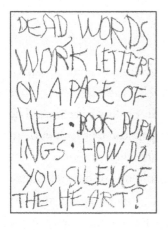

Using blood red along with jet black pages from magazines and my own paper collection, I shredded the pages and glued them down. Then I scrawled my feelings out in words. After the rage, I encountered grief. Without intending to, I created a huge, raw vagina shape. I realized then that my books are like my children. I felt like a woman whose child is stillborn. In this case, it had been ripped away from me through someone else's decision. Tearing the paper was a way to ritualize my explosive feelings: shock, frustration, help-lessness, and grief. Most of all, I felt rage at the way the whole thing was handled.

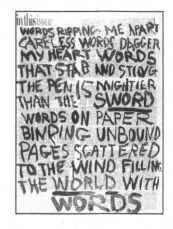

Doing the collage helped me clear my body, my emotions, and my head so that I could decide what to do next. I took the action I needed to take and was able to function in a businesslike manner. The book never went back into print, but I was able to carry on and write more books. Most of all, I was deeply grateful for the collage medium. It helped me honor my pain and some difficult but very legiti-mate feelings in the best way I know how.

LET IT RIP

Materials

Art paper, scissors, glue, magazines with photos, drawing materials (as above), journal and felt pens, colored paper (such as construction paper)

Activity

1. Place your art materials next to the art paper and start going through magazines for colors, images, and words that express anger (or any feelings in this family of emotions). If anger is up for you right now, express it. If not, remember a time when you did feel angry about something in order to pour it out through the art materials.

2. Tear or cut images and shapes from your magazines and stack of colored paper. Glue the torn elements onto the art paper. If you wish, write your feelings in words, phrases, or graffiti around your collage.

3. Sit quietly and observe your feelings after completing the collage. How do you feel now? Write about it in your journal using your *nondominant hand.*

Feeling scattered

In today's complex world a common complaint is that we *feel scattered,* or we're *going in too many directions.* We say, I can't seem to *get it together* or I'm *coming apart at the seams.* Collage is a wonderful medium for exploring these emotions. Ritualizing these feelings by actually cutting up bits and pieces of paper or fabric can help you experience chaos or fragmentation in a new way. A lot of pieces of paper strewn on your desk may not look like anything, but when you arrange them on your art paper to express a feeling, a whole new order of meaning emerges. Try it for yourself.

Bits and Pieces

Repeat the "let it rip" activity above, this time focusing on what it's like to feel scattered, going off in all directions, or fragmented. Again, choose colors and make shapes that best express these scattered feelings. You may even find magazine photographs that actually portray this condition directly, perhaps a picture of someone who is obviously scattered. Include these in your collage.

If you aren't feeling this way right now, go back to a recent time when you did feel such an emotion. On the other hand, if this is how you are feeling, let it out onto the page.

When nothing makes sense: chaos, confusion, and ambivalence

I took one page from a magazine and tore it up, scattering it all over my art paper. It really helped me to see how I do this in my life. It happens when I lack focus and fail to set priorities. I take on too much, *going in all directions*, and then have this emotional reaction of feeling like I'm *coming apart*.

In a predominantly left-brain world that praises logic and intellectual thinking, accepting feelings (which are nonrational) is not easy. This is especially true of muddy, murky feelings like confusion and ambivalence, which are hard to get a handle on and difficult to articulate. We prefer things to be clear-cut, straightforward, and rational. Emotions that ramble around in seemingly chaotic ways make many of us very uncomfortable. Anger, sadness, and fear are a little easier to identify, but whether or not we accept them is another matter. Embracing *all* our feelings includes allowing things like chaos, confusion, and ambivalence to have their say as well. Since it's often difficult to put these feelings into words, the visual arts are a wonderful doorway for accessing them.

Torn Apart

Repeat the "let it rip" activity above, but focus only on chaos, confusion, and ambivalence.

As mentioned earlier, certain art media have a way of coaxing out particular emotions. Part of it has to do with the physical experience you have when using that medium. As you saw above, if you feel torn, then actually tearing things apart can help in releasing these emotions. An equally important factor is the very nature of the medium itself. Certainly it is possible to express any feeling with any art materials, but some seem more satisfying and effective than others. I refer to this as matching the medium to the mood. It will differ for each individual. You might prefer expressing chaos with a black crayon whereas someone else may use several contrasting colors or shapes.

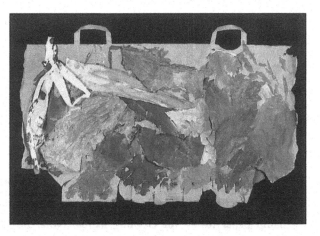

One woman expressed conflict by tearing a big brown grocery bag down the side, flattening it out and using it as background for her collage. She tore shapes and glued them down and also painted the torn pieces as well as the background paper. Her palette of colors included lots of blacks, greens, dark blues, and grays, with some red-and-white highlights.

Just as we feel things differently, we all see things differently. The media being presented here are simply suggestions. By all means, if another set of materials calls out to you as the right vehicle for certain feelings, then follow your instincts. Match your mood to a medium of your choice.

Exploring pastels

Here's another medium to explore: chalk pastels. Soft and powdery, they lend themselves to blending with the fingers. They're wonderful for creating softer contours and subtle hues of color. This is a highly tactile medium because it can be approached directly with your hands on the paper. As the chalk powders up and gets on your hands, you can actually rub the color into the paper. This ability to blend colors makes chalk pastel a wonderful medium for expressing more subtle and subdued emotions. Chalk pastels are a little messy, so if you're trying to express messy feelings, they are very appropriate. In the end, you really need to experience it for yourself. So let's do the next activity.

FOGGY FEELINGS

Materials

Art paper and soft chalk pastels in assorted colors, spray fixative or inexpensive hair spray to set the finished drawing (prevents it from rubbing off on other things), slightly damp paper towels for cleaning hands (Note: Be sure the art paper has an absorbent surface. Shiny or glossy paper won't work because the pastel won't stick to it. For instance, some photocopy paper is too slick and too thin; construction paper has a better surface.)

Activity

1. Place your art materials next to the art paper and select some colors that express chaos, confusion, ambivalence. If none of these words says it for you, go to the Directory of Emotions and find the one(s) that fit.

2. As you draw, observe the properties of the medium and the colors.

   - What kinds of lines can you make to express this feeling?
   - What shapes reflect this emotion?
   - How can you blend the colors with your fingers and hands? Stay true to your feelings and let them speak through the pastels.

3. After completing your drawing, sit quietly and look at it. What do you see? How do you feel?

Painting your feelings

Another medium for exploring the family of feelings related to chaos, confusion, and ambivalence is watercolor. Since you can mix colors and blend them, a box of a dozen colors or more will suffice. You'll find that watercolor is difficult to control. By its very nature, water wants to run all over the place. The more water you use with it, the more it seems to have a mind of its own. It just doesn't want to stay put. What a great metaphor for feelings of confusion. They wander around mysteriously inside, not wanting to be nailed down and not easy to name. Watercolor is like that: It asks for you to be spontaneous, go with the flow, be flexible and improvise.

If one color bleeds into another and a messy area results, then perhaps you can just observe that and let it be. Watercolor tests your ability to accept what is. It will also reflect soft and subtle feelings in very poetic ways. So have fun flowing with this beautifully fluid medium. It has a lot to teach you about life. Think of it as a meditation.

FLOWING WITH FEELING

Materials

Art paper, box of watercolors (in individual pans or tubes) with twelve colors or more, brush, jar of water, paper towels to dry the brush and dampen the paper (Note: Be sure the art paper has an absorbent surface. Shiny or glossy paper won't work because the watercolor won't absorb into it.)

Activity

1. Place your art materials next to the art paper.
2. Dampen one square of paper towel and rub it around gently on the surface of your paper. Then begin painting your feelings out onto the slightly wet paper. Use your *nondominant hand.* Express a feeling from the family of emotions we've been discussing. Is it ambivalence? Confusion? Again, if none of these words says it for you, go to the Directory of Emotions and find one that does.
3. Allow yourself to explore the fluid nature of this medium and the colors that are unique to it. Adding more or less water will lighten or brighten the

When I contemplated messiness and chaos, the thought of dirty hands came to mind. I painted the palm of one hand with a rusty earth color and started blotting it on the paper. It felt great to mess around. As the paint started drying, I went back and painted the silhouette of my hands on the paper. More feelings of messiness. After cleaning my hands off to change colors, I superimposed more hand and finger prints using dark blue and white. It gave me a whole new perspective on chaos and messiness. I'm usually pretty fastidious in daily life, so it surprised me that I really liked doing this picture. And I even like the end result.

colors. You can also mix colors. Make as many pictures as you like. Apply the paint to your hands and blot your hands and fingers on the art paper, creating a printed picture of the emotion.

4. Sit quietly and observe your feelings after completing the painting(s). What was the process like? How do you feel now?

Alternative

Finger paints can be used as well. I'd suggest doing that at a later time. If you decide to try them, you'll probably want paper that is better suited to finger paint (shiny and smoother). Finger paints are thick, wet, and messy, and paper that is made for finger painting is usually quite slick so that the paint will stay on the surface and not absorb too quickly.

Scared stiff: fear

Fear is one of the most basic and pervasive of all emotions. It drives many of our actions and reactions to the world around us. Fear can save lives. If it becomes chronic, it can ruin lives. I've talked to victims of armed robbery who attribute their survival to fear. The thought of confronting or fighting with the criminals never entered their minds. They were simply too terrified. Many who resist in such situations are killed or injured. Terror in the face of natural disasters or accidents is also a normal reaction. Our fear prompts us to run for cover and protect ourselves. Friends and family members of mine who survived the 1994 Los Angeles–area earthquake and its aftershocks still speak of the gut-wrenching fear they felt. The combination of terror and gut instinct impelled them to shield themselves from furnishings, china, and pictures that were crashing all around them the night of the big quake. They found safe shelter under tables, in alcoves, in closets, and in all sorts of nooks and crannies they'd never thought of as protective.

We all carry our own set of fears: snakes and spiders, air travel, the dentist's drill, the boss's tantrums, job loss, death, public speaking, bankruptcy, illness, and aging.

Stop for a moment and ask yourself: What are my biggest fears? What things, situations, or people scare me the most?

In addition to the big fears, there are also the chronic worries we carry around inside every day. Instead of practicing the power of positive thinking, we create negative affirmations with our imaginations. Staying chronically in this worried, fretful frame of mind can be lethal. Worry-induced stress is definitely not good for our bodies or our minds. Obsessing about worst-case scenarios in the future and stewing about what could happen make it difficult to live creatively in the present. Instead we inhabit a no-man's-land that doesn't exist. The longer we hang out in our negative thoughts, the more likely we are to actually create a self-fulfilling prophecy. And we know that worry generates a toxic chemical reaction in the body, as well as fear.

Like all our emotions, fear has something to teach us. Whether it's a response to a crisis or a chronic attitude, fear can be the royal road to learning trust and courage. It has brought many people closer to God and even inspired nonbelievers to investigate the possibility of a higher power. In the following mixed-media activity, you will explore the many faces of fear and find lessons in one of the most painful and challenging of emotions.

What Fear Looks Like

Repeat the "let it rip" activity above (p. 89), but this time focus your attention on what it's like to feel afraid. This time, you may want to include other media besides collage, such as painting and drawing.

I chose a gray paper to work on. Fear feels gray to me, like dark, foreboding clouds. I started by intentionally tearing paper off the border of the page. When I'm nervous and afraid, I often tear up paper napkins without realizing what I'm doing until later.

With crayons and paint, I made a person in a fetal position. I felt my fear as a kind of shrinking, turning in on myself—a need to protect myself. I created some protection by gluing down the paper I'd torn from the border in a ring around the figure. I also painted on and around it with black. After this wall of protection was finished, it looked to me like those cir-

cular barbed-wire fence tops they put around prisons. The barbed wire protects me, but I could also be a prisoner of my own fear. I felt a lot better after doing the collage.

Feeling down: depression, sadness, and grief

Feeling down and blue are emotions that we all go through at one time or another. If we think we're supposed to be happy all the time, then these families of emotions will definitely present a problem. We'll hide them or deny even having such feelings. Forcing a happy face when we're really feeling melancholy can cause these feelings to go underground.

There are many situations in our lives that evoke sadness and grief. The death of a loved one, the loss of a job, the end of a relationship, relocation, saying good-bye to a familiar place and lifestyle. Sometimes we even need to grieve the end of an era: graduation from school, the end of a project, the accomplishment of a goal. For even though we have experienced success, saying farewell to the process that got us there is not easy. We miss the people, the activities, the challenge of striving to accomplish our desired result. Sometimes we don't even know we're grieving until we start exploring our feelings through art.

Art is valuable for those who know they have something to be sad about. These emotions come in waves. You may have thought you'd cried every last tear over the loss of a relationship or a loved one, yet suddenly the grief resurfaces. It's important to allow the feelings to be, without questioning them or trying to make them go away. In grief support groups and bereavement work in counseling, the arts provide a wonderful vehicle for truly embracing grief and allowing it to show. Sometimes in sharing such images with those we trust, we can open ourselves to the empathy and compassion of others.

On the flip side of the coin, we need to understand that staying stuck in sadness for long periods of time can damage our health: Depression, sadness, and loneliness are some of the feelings that have been shown to release stress-producing chemicals into the body. A better way to deal with them is to feel them, heal them, and let them move through. In doing this, we're not trying to make them disappear. Quite the opposite. Expressing these feelings through the arts lets them appear before our eyes, to be seen and acknowledged.

Revisiting earlier activities

Whether your sadness is in response to a current situation or has become chronic, you can use the same media you already explored above for honoring these darker, gloomier emotions. I recommend applying all of the activities described in this chapter. You can go through the activities one at a time or select the medium you think will best express your particular feelings.

- Draw out the blues.
- Paint when you're feeling down, mixing colors to match your mood.
- Find magazine pictures that reflect depression or sadness and make a collage.
- Look at your artwork and do some insight writing in your journal.

Trust your intuition. Go with it. Remember, life is a rainbow. It has all colors and all feelings. Liberate them through visual arts.

Helplessness and vulnerability

In a world that idolizes power, feelings of helplessness and vulnerability are frowned on. This is especially true in the business world and in many organizations and insti-

tutions. When our most sensitive soft spots are carefully camouflaged, we hide an important aspect of ourselves. In hiding our vulnerability, we put on a mask of invulnerability. We insulate ourselves from each other and stay away from the most tender places in our heart, for love is born of empathy and compassion, and compassion is born of pain.

When we reveal our weakest spots, we allow them to heal. It has been said that we are strongest in the broken places. It is in embracing those broken places that we can also find our true inner strength.

If emotions are teachers, perhaps this family of feelings is the greatest teacher of all. In twelve-step programs, the first step is recognition that one's individual ego self is powerless over the addictive substance or behavior. That eventually leads to reaching out to the group for help but, most important, to a higher power within. Throughout history, religious conversions and spiritual breakthroughs have grown out of the fertile soil of anguish and vulnerability. Fairy tales and myths speak to the magic of breaking through the darkest obstacles. The heroes and heroines are usually weak and vulnerable children facing giants, witches, and other seemingly overpowering odds. These trials and tribulations always lead to the light. The great storyteller J.R.R. Tolkien writes about this. He says that there is a pivotal moment in every great tale when things are darkest, yet that is precisely when something magical occurs, "wider than the walls of the world." What an elegant image! And therein lies the lesson. Beyond our limited perception, there is something "wider than the walls of this world," waiting for us to see it. On the other side of darkness, there is light.

Vulnerability (along with sadness and grief) takes us to our knees. And it is on our

---

Revisiting Earlier Activities

Vulnerability and feelings of helplessness can be expressed in several media. I suggest looking back at the activities with which you have already acquainted yourself. Start using your own innate intuitive ability to match the medium to your mood. Ask yourself, "Which medium would work best for conveying this emotion right now?" Look at the possibilities, and consider mixing media, if that seems right.

- Draw with pastels or felt pens
- Paint with watercolors
- Make a collage
- Mix the media
- Write about these feelings in your journal, using whichever hand you like

Colors are important, but so is size. Many people find that a small piece of paper works best for expressing feelings of weakness or vulnerability. As you select the medium, ask yourself about what size feels appropriate. One woman did a tiny painting that she called *Diminished,* consisting of a colored dot within a circle placed right in the center of a very small art board. She purposely chose a very small leftover piece of art board, and within that she used only a tiny portion of the page to portray feeling diminished.

knees that we may finally come to prayer, to thanksgiving, and to honoring what is darkest as well what is lightest in us. What is human and also divine.

At home with yourself: happiness, love, and playfulness

We began this chapter by exploring emotions that people have disowned the most and have the most difficulty expressing in a safe, productive way. In therapy these are the feelings that clients often need help embracing: anger, confusion, fear, loneliness, sadness, helplessness, and hurt. In workshops, these are the emotions that come up over and over again. These emotions are a great gift, for they deepen and ripen us. They age us in the sense that good wine or cheese is aged. The paradox is that when we embrace the pain, chaos, and bewilderment, we are exercising the very emotional muscles that enable us to feel peace, joy, and love. From plunging to the depths of our soul, we are then free to fly to the heights. After the night comes the day, and accordingly we first feel grief and then joy. By avoiding the tough stuff, we numb ourselves to all feeling. Golda Meir once said that if you can't cry with your whole heart, you cannot laugh, either. Expressing the very feelings we most shy away from empowers us to be more wholly human and experience true aliveness.

In the film *City of Angels,* Nicholas Cage's character, Seth, is a celestial being who has not been cooked in the stew of human emotions and physical experience. Although in a perpetual peaceful state, he longs to participate in the human condition. Through an act of free will he jumps and falls into what the Sufis call the privilege of being human. After a bliss-filled day with the woman he loves, played by Meg Ryan, he loses her to death in a sudden accident. Afterward he is asked by another celestial being if he would have become human had he known the outcome. He replies with an emphatic yes. He would have done it all again. Just one breath of her hair, one kiss was enough.

When we attune to the inner self through the expressive arts, the peace and love we find for ourselves are truly awesome. Art becomes meditation and prayer. Kent had been suffering from chronic fatigue syndrome to such a degree that he had to stop working as a counselor and teacher. A highly creative individual, Kent took up photography and art during his illness. He uncovered vast tracts of uncharted disowned emotions within: feelings never felt and emotions never expressed. Kent discovered playfulness and joy. He began by finding them buried in his body. As he unraveled his emotions through drawing and writing, a powerful creative voice emerged. A new life and new career were born. Having avoided intimate commitment all his life, he was finally able to marry and now enjoys a happy family life.

Activities

All of the media you've explored above are appropriate for expressing this family of emotions, which includes happiness, love, and playfulness. If you need to find another word that says it for you, turn to the Directory of Emotions. Then find the medium of expression that seems most suitable for your particular feeling. To review, the media presented above are:

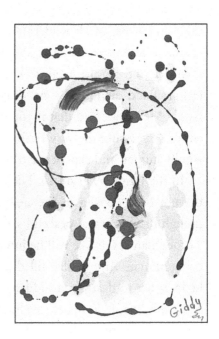

- drawing with crayons, oil, or chalk pastels
- collage
- watercolor painting
- insight writing in your journal

Expressive arts as meditation: peace, contentment, and serenity

Visual art is an ancient form of meditation. It is used for contemplation, as in the Tibetan Buddhist thangka banners, Hindu yantra paintings, calligraphic scrolls hung over devotional altars in Asian homes, and statues of holy beings in both the Catholic and Hindu traditions. The mandala that appears in such exquisite examples as the rose window in Gothic cathedrals has been found throughout history and in all cultures as a motif for worship and centering. One of my favorite forms of art as spiritual practice is the Asian tradition called zenga. Artist monks and nuns create calligraphic scrolls with inspirational words and brush paintings for use in meditation. It is believed that the artists and some of their devotees attain enlightenment through creating or contemplating these works of art.

The ability to surrender to the medium and not know what the outcome will be is particularly appropriate when accessing feelings of peace and serenity. In letting go of control and allowing the process, we surrender to life.

Watercolor, especially with Japanese or Chinese calligraphy brushes, is very well suited to expressing tranquillity and peacefulness. It is even richer when combined with chalk pastels that can be blended into the dampened paper. Crayon resist, in which drawing with crayons is followed by watercolor painting, is also a medium that lends itself to expressing these emotions.

Collage is another wonderful medium for exploring peace, serenity, and contentment. In your magazines, find photographs that express these feelings. Your collage can also serve as a visual affirmation of these feelings when used as a poster displayed on your wall. Keep looking at it every day; it will lighten up your life.

Any of the media you have used so far can be used for expressing peace, contentment, and serenity. Meditative painting or drawing is best done with your nondominant hand. The same goes for insight writing. Review the following media and pick the one that attracts you:

- drawing with crayons or oil or chalk pastels
- watercolor
- collage (using both hands)
- mixed media
- insight writing

PEACE BE TO YOU

Materials

Art paper, box of watercolors with twelve colors or more, brush, jar of water, paper towels to dry the brush, chalk or oil pastels, journal, and felt pens

Optional: Japanese or Chinese calligraphy brush in small or medium size

Recorded meditation music of your choice. I use the following:

- *Music for Zen Meditation and Other Joys* (clarinet, koto, shakuhachi) (Tony Scott, Shinichi Yuze, Hozan Yamamoto)
- *Canyon Trilogy: Native American Flute Music* (R. Carlos Nakai)
- *Sunlit Reverie: Flute Music* (Radhika Miller)

Activity

1. Place your art materials next to the art paper.
2. Dampen one square of paper towel and rub it gently on the surface of your paper. Then with your *nondominant hand*, begin painting your feelings out onto the slightly wet paper. Express a feeling from the family of emotions we've been discussing: peace, serenity, contentment. Again, if none of these words says it for you, go to the Directory of Emotions and find one that does. As you paint, contemplate the word.

3. Allow yourself to explore the fluid nature of this medium and let it take you where it wants to go. Let go of preconceived ideas and allow the music to flow through you as you paint.

4. Make another painting using both hands. This time don't dampen the paper. Instead, put a brush in your *nondominant hand* and another one in your *dominant hand.* Let them paint at the same time. If you only have one brush, then draw with your *dominant hand*, using a chalk or oil pastel, and paint with your *nondominant hand.* Let your hands play together on the paper. Think of it as dancing with yourself.

5. Sit quietly and observe your feelings after completing the painting(s). What was the process like? How do you feel now? You may want to write about it in your journal, using your *nondominant hand.*

Embracing happiness: joy, enthusiasm, and creativity

Why do we strive to achieve our goals? Why do we pursue our heart's desires? Why do we go on vacations? Because we want to experience happiness. For instance, recreation and renewal are big business! Cruises, weekend getaway packages, and day spas all promise that we'll come back feeling like a new person. In the humdrum of daily duties, work, and chores, it is easy to lose the enthusiasm we started out with as children. Like artistic expression itself, joy is our birthright, but we lose it over the years. Somewhere in the business of growing up, the light gets dimmer and dimmer. When Roberto Benigni accepted his Oscars for *Life Is Beautiful,* the whole world watched in amazement as this child-in-a-man's-body leaped over theater seats and scaled the apron of the stage to receive his award. Love, enthusiasm, and joy bursting forth in the midst of jaded, star-studded opulence. Hollywood had never seen anything quite like it. His joy was so great, it confounded people.

If you want to see a film that is packed with joy, enthusiasm, and creativity, rent the video of *Big,* starring Tom Hanks. When his wish to become big comes true, a little boy named Josh finds himself in a man's body. The life of an adult is suddenly thrust on him, but he's still a little kid inside. There are some scenes in this movie that are guaranteed to bring out the child in everyone. Get ready to laugh and cry and have a rollicking time. If you've already seen the movie, try viewing it again. There are so many details that get lost the first time.

Activities

All of the media from previous activities in this chapter are suited to expressing these emotions. All you have to do is replace the theme of the original activity with a word that says happiness, joy, enthusiasm, creativity, or whatever you like.

These emotions are also wonderful themes for making a photo collage of your life dreams. Use your imagination and create your heart's desire in a collage poster that you can use as your evening star to navigate through your life. This is your visual affirmation of the experiences you want in life. For more detailed guidance on how to create the life you want, see my book *Visioning: Ten Steps to Designing the Life of Your Dreams*.

PIECES OF A DREAM

Materials

Art paper, collage materials, magazines, journal, and felt pens

Recorded music: *Music for the Mozart Effect, Volume III, Unlock the Creative Spirit*, compiled and sequenced by Don Campbell; *The Sound of Feelings* by Jessie Allen Cooper; or music from your own collection

Activity
1. Place your art materials next to the art paper.
2. Contemplate a word that describes one of the family of feelings above: joy, happiness, and enthusiasm. Create a collage of images that expresses the feeling you are focusing on.
3. Sit quietly and look at your finished collage. What was the process like? How do you feel now?

Try a little tenderness: love

Love is something we most long for, try to recapture, and spend much of our lives attempting to create. If we feel we don't have it, love is a wonderful subject to meditate on. Simply contemplating times when we loved and felt loved can open us up to love as a living element in our lives. Expressing feelings of love, nurturing, and tenderness through the arts is a wonderful way to own these emotions. Instead of thinking we are empty and desperately looking for someone outside to make us feel loved, we go inward and find that it was there all the time.

I have known students and clients who manifested a loving relationship with another by first contemplating what such a relationship would feel like. They did this through art, especially collage and journal writing. By activating these feelings within, they drew to themselves people who were on the same wavelength.

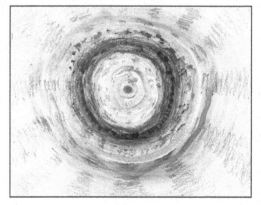

Love

What does love look like to you? What would a more loving life be like? What would a loving relationship be? How would your life be different? Use the arts to portray your vision of love.

Activities

All the media in this chapter are suited to expressing love. Simply change the theme of the original activity to a word that expresses love, nurturance, trust, affection, tenderness, or whatever theme feels right to you.

Free

5. SCULPTED FEELINGS: MAD, SAD, AND GLAD

In this chapter, we explore feelings three-dimensionally through the sculptural medium of clay. All of us can expand our ability to make the invisible inner world of feelings visible in the outer world. Poet Gerard Manley Hopkins used the term "inscape" to describe this form of revelation of the unseen. The artist feels an emotional charge and seeks to capture the power of that experience by translating it into material form. In expressive arts we do the same thing. For instance, in visual and sculptural arts, we act on matter. Transferring our emotions into the raw materials, we shape and reshape until we've outwardly embodied what we felt inwardly. Yes, there is the art piece, but there is also the dance that created it. With every movement of our bodies, we are also enacting our feelings.

As we found with two-dimensional arts, certain emotions want to be expressed with gestures and motions that convey the very nature of that feeling. This is nothing new; we do it all the time in everyday life. An angry or frustrated man pounds his fist on a tabletop. A woman who has been frightened or traumatized sits all hunched over, her arms and hands clasped, as if protecting her heart and other vital organs. We call this body language. It is the unconscious dance of feelings expressing through our posture and actions. And the body doesn't lie.

In the last two chapters you saw how making art on paper can allow emotions to be released. Just as important, you saw the connection between art making and the body. The very act of putting marks and shapes on the page requires a series of movements engaging our bones, muscles, and nerves—our whole body—as well as our heart, mind, and instincts.

Just as the medium matches the mood, so does the movement. This is not to say that people are conscious of their movements while engaged in expressive art making. Most of the time, the gestures just happen, as in everyday life. They are a by-product of the emotion trying to get out. An angry person doesn't have to think about frowning. She gets mad and her face automatically goes into that expression. It is the same with a smile. When emotional energy is in motion, it does its own dance.

Sometimes we actually do become aware of the movement we are making as the art takes shape. One workshop participant laughed uproariously as she scribbled and made graffiti with a big fat kindergarten crayon, ripping a hole in the newsprint paper. As her resentment burst forth onto the page, this usually withdrawn woman declared, "Wow, it feels great to really press hard with this crayon. It's empowering!" After a few moments she added, in a tone of surprise, "The tension in my shoulders is gone! I must have had a really big chip on my shoulder." She laughed. "But I think I dumped it on this paper."

Later, this woman told me that she had been an unwanted child. Her mother was unwed and had been abandoned by the father as soon as he learned she was pregnant. The mother attempted an abortion, which failed. Then she had abused her daughter emotionally and physically throughout her childhood. As a result, this woman had grown up being afraid to *have a voice* or *make her mark in the world.* Apologetic for being born in the first place, she'd become a wallflower, receding into the background where she felt safe and out of harm's way. The scribble drawing opened up a creative vent through which she could express her true self. She then went on to work in clay. Using the activities presented in this chapter, she turned her life around. Setting up a studio in her home, she continued sculpting in clay, releasing rage, fear, grief, as well as playfulness and creativity. She even went on to take dance classes, something she'd always been too timid to do. After a year, she was a new and vibrant woman, hardly recognizable from the shy, frightened person who came to the first workshop.

In matching the medium to the mood, we want to involve the whole self in the expressive act. When it comes to the visual and sculptural arts, there is probably no better medium for total body involvement than clay. Wet, slippery, heavy lumps of clay invite you to interact with them in a very physical way—that is the nature of the material. The earth is asking to be worked and kneaded, manipulated and enjoyed.

In observing clients and students who are totally lost in the clay experience, I've often wondered what it is that draws people into clay so completely. Almost without exception, they escape their worries and become silent and word-free as they enter this most primitive of all media. An almost sacred atmosphere of reverence descends on the room as warm-up preparations begin. Getting to know the clay is a very intimate experience for many, as they explore how receptive and malleable and just plain fun this material is. Some even get teary, as if they are coming back home. Perhaps we are returning, through what Jung called the collective unconscious, to our ancestral dwellings in caves, to those first art studios deep in the bowels of the earth.

After our initial contemplation of the clay, we swing into action. One thing about clay is that you can do so much with it and to it. You can pull, push, roll, squeeze, punch, slap, hit, pinch, pound, tear, cut, scratch, beat, and swat. You can poke, dig, compress, and flatten it, as well as hollow it out and coil it. You can also caress, pat, stroke, knead, hollow, shape, and build with it. Clay lends itself to heavy, massive forms, yet it can just as easily be manipulated into delicate, thin-walled contours. You can dump your anger into clay, but you can also create enclosures and protective forts. Tenderness, sensuality, and erotic feelings also lend themselves to full expression in this medium. Much to the surprise of many clients and students, genital forms often emerge from the clay, not consciously intended. As you allow your hands to simply be with the clay, many discoveries emerge—about yourself and the medium.

Preparing the clay, preparing yourself

Before exploring emotions directly with the clay, it is important to prepare the materials and yourself. I'll help you enter the spirit of the clay and the unique qualities of this medium through a sensory awareness meditation. Keep in mind that every hunk of clay has its own unique properties. In order to get to know this particular piece of clay, you will need to stay in the moment and in the experience. That's why I call it a clay meditation. If one of the benefits of meditation is the quieting of the chattering mind, the experience of being here now, then clay is a wonderful vehicle for achieving that state. It commands your attention.

Find a place to do this work, such as a kitchen, garage workroom, or other room that is appropriate for messier activities. Some suggestions are:

- kitchen table
- table on a back porch or deck
- counter in a garage or hobby room
- workshop area

Before beginning, I'd like you to contemplate these words from the classic book by M. C. Richards, *Centering: In Pottery, Poetry, and the Person*. Read them as a prayer or invocation. Ask your Creative Self to bestow "the generosity to let a thing be what it is, the patience to come to know it, a sense of the mystery in all living things, and a joy in new experiences."

CLAY MEDITATION

Materials

Gray or red terra cotta clay.* Work surface, such as a wooden or Masonite board (smooth side up). You can also use a plastic tarp covering a tabletop or a very thick piece of corrugated cardboard. To the side of your work surface place a bowl of warm water for moistening your hands. Also include paper towels and trash container or old rags for cleanup. Smock, old shirt, or apron to protect clothes. Large plastic airtight container with lid (like ones used for storing foods in refrigerator) to store the used piece of clay for reuse later. Note: You may want to read the guided meditation that follows into a tape recorder so that you can play it back and follow it while working with the clay.

Activity

1. Getting to know the clay: Sit or stand comfortably in front of the clay, which is placed in the center of your work surface. Place your hands on the clay without doing anything to it. Allow yourself to relax by focusing on your breathing. Let your breath come in and out in a slow steady flow. Think of the ocean's tides and get into an even rhythm. As you inhale, imagine the energy of the earth coming up through the soles of your feet and filling your whole body and mind. On the exhale, let any tensions shed back down into the earth.

2. Now immerse your hands in the bowl of warm water that is to the side of your work area. Let your hands remain there for a while and enjoy the sensation of warmth.

*Get self-hardening terra cotta ceramic clay that does not need to be fired in a kiln. It can be bought inexpensively at art supply stores in twenty-five-pound rectangular blocks that come in sealed plastic bags. The block of clay resembles a huge loaf of bread. Cut off a large slab about a thumb's length in thickness by pulling a piece of twine, heavy string, or wire right through the big block of clay. Each piece will look like a giant slice of bread.

Then pick up the hunk of clay in front of you and hold it in your hands. Become aware of the feel of the clay: the weight, smell, dryness or wetness, and texture.

3. Placing the clay on the work surface again, close your eyes. Slowly begin running your moistened hands over its surface. Be receptive to the form of the clay in its present state. Get to know it. Don't try to mold, shape, or change it. Rather experience the form that already exists. Accept it as it is right now, simply feeling it by running your hands and fingers gently all over the surface. Feel the smooth places and the rough places, the wetness and the warmth or coolness of the different parts of the clay. Feel its contours, depressions, lumps, and bumps. If the clay gets dry, wet your hands some more. Continue feeling the clay, but now open your eyes and notice all the contours and textures. Do this for as long as you like. When you feel finished, go to the next step.

4. Exploring the clay actively: Become aware of your hands as active agents, the clay as passive and receptive. Close your eyes again. Begin working your fingers into the clay. Let your hands do what they feel like doing. Is the clay hard or soft? Stiff or pliable? Do your hands want to pound, flatten, grasp, or poke it? Do they want to caress, stroke, or hold it? Or do they want to squeeze, pinch, or tear the clay to pieces? Do they want to mold, dig, or build with it? Let your hands interact with the clay in any way that feels good to them. There is no right or wrong way to do this. Your hands will know what the clay is calling them to do. Follow your instincts and let your hands take the lead. Continue doing this for as long as you wish.

5. Creating the self: Let your hands begin to form the clay, repeating to yourself the phrase: "This clay is me and I am creating myself. I am always the same, yet constantly changing." Your eyes are still closed, and your hands are still taking the lead. Do not try to imagine what the clay looks like. Just let your hands do all the work. The only thing to be concerned about is whether the forms being made feel good to your hands. Continue doing this for as long as you like, keeping your eyes closed all of the time.

6. When you feel finished, stop working and open your eyes to see what you have made. Look at the clay piece from all angles.

- What do you see? What was it like to work on this clay?
- Did any emotions come up? Any memories? Any associations with other experiences?
- Did any self-criticism surface about your artistic abilities, etc.?
- How do you feel about what came out of the clay?

Finally, run your fingers and hands around the finished piece without changing it. Look at it and feel it at the same time.

Note: Sometimes people create a piece that they really want to contemplate, journal about, and use for more personal growth work. If that becomes true, then put the finished clay piece out in the sun or let it air dry and harden at room temperature. Whether you save any of the clay pieces you make in this chapter is up to you. It is not necessary to keep them, as the *process* is most important here.

Getting to know the clay (person working with clay with eyes shut)

7. If you are not saving your piece of clay, gather it up and form it into a ball. If you are stopping with this activity, place your clay ball in a storage container or airtight bag for reuse. If you want to continue, use the clay again for the next activity.

Comments about the process

The clay is a great metaphor for life. It changed so much as I worked with it. At first it was hard, stiff, unyielding, and difficult to shape. It softened, though, as I worked it, and became pliable, more plastic, and easy to move.

All these pieces come together to make a whole. The shapes seem to be the same (round, receptive, or closed off), but there's variety. Some want to clump together, others want to sit open. Some feel soft and flowing, others are sticky and stiff. It seems that there are many separate parts to me and the whole—it is complex. But all of them—open, closed, hard, or soft—are important parts to me and the life I'm creating.

After I finished the piece, I started feeling it with my eyes open. I didn't change it, I just saw it with both my eyes and my hands at the same time. I'd pictured it with my eyes closed while making it, then looked at it with my eyes open. But feeling it and seeing it at the same time was a very different experience. I noticed what parts drew my hands toward them.

The hot emotions: anger, sexuality, and passion

From the list of action words describing the nature of clay play, it was pretty obvious which emotions would easily express themselves through this medium. When you picture verbs like pushing, poking, punching, slapping, hitting, pinching, pounding, tearing, and beating, you probably visualize people expressing anger. Words like caress, pat, stroke, and knead, on the other hand, evoke images of love and nurturing: people making love, expressing affection to a person or pet, or making bread to feed others.

We'll begin with anger, sexuality, and passion. I put these in the family of what I call the hot emotions. They are usually associated with high energy and are often portrayed in drawing and painting with warm or hot colors: red, scarlet, orange, bright pinks, or violet. When people are angry they get *hot under the collar* or *turn red with rage.* When sexually aroused, our faces often get flushed. Passion is anything but cool. It is enlivened by an emotional fire that is fueled by the feelings we feed it.

Getting down to earth

Now you will learn to harness the power of these strong emotions through the medium and movement of clay. As you play with this piece of earth, you may return to early childhood memories of making mud pies, digging in the ground, or playing with clay in preschool or kindergarten. You may also recall specific times when you would have liked to pound out your anger and frustration but had no safe place to do it. Now you do.

CAUTION: **If you had an abusive childhood, painful memories might come up during this activity. If these become overpowering for you emotionally, my advice is to get professional help. You may need some counseling for dealing with emotion-charged wounds of the past before you can continue working with the hot emotions on your own.**

The following activities will give you the tools needed to accept and release your hot emotions in a safe way. Instead of being thrown out of control by these strong, hot feelings, you can now own them. We say we have a feeling, and that's how it should be: to have an emotion, rather than the emotion having us; to be the equestrian who rides the horse of raw, primitive feelings, instead of being thrown to the ground by one's mount. In acting your rage and embodying it in clay, you also allow strong and often frightening emotions to shape-shift into whatever form they take, into whatever emotion is coming up next. For instance, once your anger has had a chance to come out, it may turn into peace or a feeling of freedom. In this way, you engage fully in a passionate life, allowing the entire range of emotions to be part of your experience.

Many people have asked me, why clay? Why not use a bat, tennis racket, or punching bag to release anger? The answer is that after you've screamed, hit, and punched out your anger with these objects, there's no physical vehicle to carry it further. Clay, on the other hand, can take you wherever your feelings are leading you. It is a totally neutral material. You may start with rageful pounding on the clay only to end with sadness and a lyrical sculpture that pays homage to loneliness or loss. Try doing that with a punching bag or a tennis racket.

Emotions are often like those Russian nesting dolls. Inside one there is another one, and inside that one another one still. When allowed to live and breathe naturally, feelings change from moment to moment. Clay is a wonderful mirror of what's going on inside you. The clay transforms as your feelings do.

THE SHAPE OF FEELINGS

Materials

Gray or red terra cotta clay. Work surface, such as a wooden or Masonite board (smooth side up) or plastic tarp covering a tabletop or a very thick piece of corrugated cardboard. A bowl of warm water for moistening your hands, paper towels, and trash container or old rags for cleanup. Smock, old shirt, or apron to protect clothes. Large plastic airtight container with lid to store the used piece of clay for reuse later.

Activity

1. As you did in the previous activity, sit or stand comfortably in front of the clay, which is in the center of your work surface. Place your hands on the clay and close your eyes. Allow yourself to relax by breathing rhythmically. Breathe the energy of the earth up through the soles of your feet, filling your whole body and mind. Exhale tensions down and out into the earth through your feet.

2. With your eyes closed, contemplate the emotion of anger. Recall the last time you felt this emotion. You may even be feeling it right now about some situation in your life. What situation triggered this feeling? Where do you feel this emotion in your body? What kind of sensation do you feel there? Is there a word that de-

scribes the particular kind of anger this situation provoked, such as mad, enraged, furious?

3. Open your eyes and, if you need to, moisten your hands. Then begin working your hands and fingers into the clay. Allow your hands to express your anger by whatever name you called it. Let the feeling flow out of you and into the clay. Use gestures and movements that really express this emotion. You have permission to do anything to the clay that you like. You can't hurt clay. Use your fingers, the flat of your hand, the back of your hand, your fist. Really feel the feelings and let them out. Remember, the clay can take it. Continue this as long as you need to until you are satisfied that the feelings have been released for now.

4. Close your eyes and allow your hands to make any shapes and forms they want to make. Let any emotions that are still there transfer themselves into the clay. After a while, open your eyes and continue working until you feel finished.

5. Look at and feel your finished piece for a while. Reflect on your experience with the clay and on the finished piece.

   • Did you feel a sense of release in step 3?
   • Was it comfortable or uncomfortable expressing this emotion?
   • What did you like about it? What didn't you like?
   • Did you observe anything about yourself and how you handled these feelings?
   • Did any other feelings come up?
   • How do you feel about the finished piece? What does it say to you?

6. Roll up the clay into a ball and return it to its airtight storage container.

Comments

The situation that came up for me was the telephone company not getting my phone connected when they said they would. They were very uncooperative and even rude. Since I need my phone to receive business calls from clients, this was more than an inconvenience. It cost me the income from the work lost.

Anger release

I noticed that anger affects my whole body. It started in one part—in my solar plexus—then it spread all over. I felt tension, heat, and contraction in my legs.

The final piece was an expression of the tremendous release I had felt from banging anger out into the clay. It said relaxation, release, expansion. I liked doing it, and I enjoy looking at the final piece.

Other Applications

You can explore any emotions you wish using the exercise above. Simply contemplate a particular feeling, then find the movements and gestures that express that particular emotion.

After expressing current emotions, you can also take steps to develop emotions and qualities you want and need. Use the clay to flex new emotional muscles.

Sexuality and sensuality

As mentioned earlier, sexual passion is one of the hot emotions. If denied or seen as a bad thing, sexuality can turn against us. It can overwhelm and frighten us or turn into obsession. Studies show that sex addicts and those who are sexually anorexic (people who avoid all sexual contact) often come from homes where sex was denied, was taboo, or where it was out of control (incest, exhibitionism, promiscuity, extramarital affairs, and so forth). In the United States, we are highly ambivalent about sex. A tradition of Puritanism mixed in with the sexual revolution of the '60s and '70s has made for strange bedfellows indeed. Our traditional values preach one thing while the media teach another. Our culture's most significant role models often fail to set healthy examples. The media are always reporting yet another authority figure caught with his or her proverbial pants down: a TV minister frequenting prostitutes, a divinity school official caught with pornography on-line, priests charged with child molestation, a female therapist convicted for having sex with clients, and our former president involved in a dramatic sex scandal.

To add to these problems, we have split sensuality from sexuality and separated emotional intimacy from pleasure. Somehow we've gotten our wires crossed. Any day's television fare attests to the fact that sex and violence have been wedded in our society to a level that might shock even the Marquis de Sade—for whom sadism was named. As a practicing therapist, I witnessed the effects of this very unhealthy atmosphere around sex, love, intimacy, and pleasure. One of the materials that proved most effective in treating individuals and couples who had lost their way sexually (and sensually) was clay, for clay lends itself so perfectly to expressions of both sexual passion and sensual pleasure. Words like caress, massage, and stroke can be used to describe gestures people make with clay.

It should be obvious from earlier exercises that clay play is a wonderful practice in sensory awareness. For that reason it is an extremely appropriate medium for sex therapy. It is no coincidence that the sex therapy pioneers, Masters and Johnson, and other clinicians who developed treatment for sexual dysfunction in the '70s, made use of sensate focus exercises, such as mutual face caress and foot massage, in order to enliven physical and emotional feelings that had gone numb. They asked couples not to attempt having intercourse for a while but to practice sensory awareness and sensual contact through these structured sensate focus exercises.

In my private practice, women clients were always relieved to know they weren't alone in wanting sensual pleasure—massage, caressing, and sensual play—to be part of lovemaking. Without it, lovemaking was incomplete and unsatisfying. For men dealing with sexual dysfunction (impotence, premature ejaculation, sexual addiction) it seemed more difficult for them to explore sensuality for intimate mutual pleasuring. Their sexual behavior was overshadowed by performance anxiety. Will I be able to have an erection? Will it last? Will I please her? With all these questions going on in their heads, how could they be in their bodies?

As an art therapist, I learned early on that if you want to get someone into their body and into the here and now, clay is almost guaranteed to do the job. It is the least cerebral medium I know. It takes people right back to kindergarten and before, back to the earth, back to their deepest feelings and most natural instincts. In this next activity, you'll be exploring attitudes about your body and your senses and sensibilities about sexuality.

CAUTION: **If you were sexually abused in childhood or have been violated as an adult, this activity may be too powerful for you emotionally. If you have not had professional help for this trauma, my advice is to get counseling before attempting this activity. Do not attempt to do this healing on your own. If you have already had therapeutic treatment for the trauma, or are in therapy now, proceed cautiously. If feelings come up that are overwhelming, stop and get help from your therapist.**

My body self

Since your relationship with others begins with your relationship with yourself, you'll begin with your own body. How do you feel about your body? Are you inside your own skin or trying to look like somebody else? Can you love and accept your own body just as it is? Sensuality starts and ends in one place: your body-mind. How you enjoy the God-given gift of your senses—hearing, seeing, tasting, touching, and smelling—also gives life and passion to sexual intimacy.

In the next activity, you will begin by exploring your feelings about your own body, first by mirroring those feelings in clay and then, ideally, by learning to accept this temple of the spirit, this human body you have been given.

ACCEPTING MYSELF

Materials

Gray or red terra cotta clay. Work surface, such as a wooden or Masonite board (smooth side up) or plastic tarp covering a tabletop or a very thick piece of corrugated cardboard. A bowl of warm water for moistening your hands, paper towels, and trash container or old rags for cleanup. Smock, old shirt, or apron to protect clothes. Large plastic airtight container with lid to store the used piece of clay for reuse later. Journal and pens.

Activity

1. Place your hands on the clay and close your eyes. Relax by breathing in the earth energy through your feet and releasing tension out on the exhale. Open your eyes and moisten your hands in warm water if you need to. Work the clay until it is warm and pliable.

2. With your eyes closed, create a form that expresses your feelings about your body. Don't think about it too much, just let your hands do all the work. They do know how you feel and will mirror back the body image you carry inside. Does the size of the clay feel right? Do you need more or less clay? Make any adjustments you need to. Your clay may take the shape of a human form or it may not. It might turn out looking like an animal, tree, or other visual metaphor or symbol. It might even have an abstract shape. Let it be whatever it is.

3. When you feel finished, take a nice deep, slow breath. Then open your eyes and look at the form that has been created. Move around and look at it from all angles.

- How do you feel about it?
- Does it reflect your feelings about your own body? In what way?
- What do you like about it? Is there anything you dislike about it?
- Do you have any observations about the process of making the clay piece?

4. Set your sculpture aside on another surface or reuse the same piece of clay by rolling it into a ball. Write about your experience in your journal.

Example

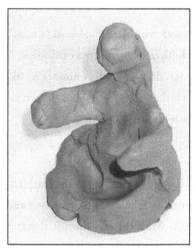

I feel comfortable with this piece that represents my feeling about my body. Congruence is the word that comes to mind. Accepting. I like the open, welcoming, receptive, soft, and warm feeling it conveys.

While making it, at first I had some thought about me making something. Then I let that thought go and let the hands move, doing what felt right to them. Then it became meditative. It was clear that my hands knew how to express the inner sense. I knew then that there was a bond between my hands and the clay. A feeling of trust came about. Whatever came out would be the truth.

In the next two-part activity you will explore your sensual self as well as your ability to be emotionally and physically intimate with another. Think of Seth, the celestial being who became human in *City of Angels*. He said he would do it all again for just one breath of her hair, just one kiss of her mouth. Just one. The Sufis call it the privilege of being human, the blessing of being able to learn the lesson of love on this planet Earth.

BEING WITH ANOTHER: PART I, SENSUALITY

Materials

Gray or red terra cotta clay. Work surface, such as a wooden or Masonite board (smooth side up) or plastic tarp covering a tabletop or a very thick piece of corrugated cardboard. A bowl of warm water for moistening your hands, paper towels, and trash container or old rags for cleanup. Smock, old shirt, or apron to protect clothes. Large plastic airtight container with lid to store the used piece of clay for reuse later.

Activity

1. Moisten your hands again in warm water if you need to. Work the clay for a while until it becomes warm and pliable.
2. Contemplate the most sensual experience you ever had. Were you out in nature, eating a delicious meal, caressing your lover, taking a hot scented bath, dancing? Close your eyes and let your sensual feelings pour out into the clay. Use gestures and movements that really express sensuality by stroking, massaging, rolling, caressing, and tenderly giving shape to the clay. Let your feelings transfer themselves into the soft, receptive clay. Allow it to take any form it wants in order to express sensuality. Continue as long as you like until you feel your expression is complete.
3. Take a nice, deep easy breath and open your eyes. Look at what you created, seeing it from the top and from all sides. Feel the finished clay piece with your fingers while looking at it, but do not change it.
4. Reflect on your experience with the clay and the finished piece.

   - Was it comfortable or uncomfortable expressing sensuality?
   - What did you like about it? What didn't you like?
   - Did any other feelings come up along with the sensuality?
   - How do you feel about the finished piece? What does it say to you?

BEING WITH ANOTHER: PART 2, SEXUALITY

Materials

Gray or red terra cotta clay. Work surface, such as a wooden or Masonite board (smooth side up) or plastic tarp covering a tabletop or a very thick piece of corrugated cardboard. A bowl of warm water for moistening your hands, paper towels, and trash container or old rags for cleanup. Smock, old shirt, or apron to protect clothes. Large plastic airtight container with lid to store the used piece of clay for reuse later. Journal and felt pens.

Activity

1. Roll up the clay into a ball and begin again. Work the clay for a while. This time your theme is sexuality.

2. Contemplate the most pleasurable sexual experience you ever had. Where were you? Who were you with? Close your eyes and let those sexual feelings pour out into the clay. Use gestures and movements that really express sexuality, letting your feelings transfer themselves into the soft, receptive clay. Allow the clay to take any form it wants for expressing sexuality. Continue as long as you like until you feel finished.

3. When you feel finished, contemplate your sculpture from all angles. Feel the finished clay piece with your fingers while looking at it, but do not change it.

   • What do you see?
   • How do you feel about it?

4. Clean your hands and write about your experiences with both parts of this activity using your *nondominant hand*. The questions in step 4 of part 1 and step 3 of part 2 can be a good springboard for your writing.

Example

> I felt comfortable expressing sensuality. I liked making an image of the feelings and the experience I was contemplating. Feeling it in my body and then making it in tangible, visible form felt peaceful. When I looked at it, my first reaction was surprise. I had no idea what it would look like. I was immersed in the tactile sensations and the sensual experience I was contemplating and expressing through the medium of clay.

Feelings of loss: grief, sadness, and loneliness

Clay often evokes deep feelings of sadness. Many clients and workshop participants have been surprised at the amount of grief that poured out while working with clay. Having their hands in this primitive material somehow unleashed emotions they didn't realize they had. One such workshop participant was Marsha, who was raising her two adopted sons as well as her second husband's two children.

At one of my weeklong Inner Child intensive workshops, Marsha did the clay meditation. During "the shape of feelings" activities, most of the group was busily releasing anger or having fun creating penises and vaginas. The energy in the room was very high, and there was quite a bit of laughter and obvious enjoyment. By contrast, Marsha seemed in a very somber mood. I could tell from her face and body language that she was experiencing some deep sadness. She had taken a piece of clay and fashioned a human form, which she later told me was a doll. It was lying on its back with its legs spread apart. She then created a snake form by rolling clay into a long coil, placing one end of the snake in the vagina between the doll's legs. Later she told me that a critical, analytical voice in her head immediately questioned why she was doing this, but she continued following my instructions and allowed her hands to create the sculpture. What her hands did next was to loop the snake coil into a large heart shape that she placed on the stomach of the doll.

Since the workshop also included Creative Journaling, Marsha then wrote down her observations. As soon as the words started flowing, so did the tears. What came up for Marsha was grief. She had undergone a hysterectomy about a year prior to the workshop. The doll with the coil heart that looked like an umbilical cord reminded her of the children she never had and never would have. She hadn't grieved the loss of her uterus or the loss of biological motherhood. Her tears were long overdue.

Repeat "the shape of feelings" activity on pages 118–19, steps 1 through 6. Instead of using anger as your theme, contemplate sadness, grief, loneliness, or any other feeling that is associated with these words.

Other Applications

- If you are feeling vulnerable and need protection (and have expressed those feelings in the clay), when you get to step 5 of "the shape of feelings" create a clay piece that embodies feeling protected and secure. One woman sculpted a child being comforted by a grown-up. A man created an abstract form being protected by a shell that resembled sea life. Another one created a hollow egg with his small, vulnerable self protected inside.
- If you are feeling frightened or timid and want to develop courage, form a clay piece that represents courage to you. Let your sculpture harden by setting it out in the sun, and use it as a totem in a place where you can see it often. By contemplating it, you reinforce the feeling and eventually embody it in yourself. If you can express it in clay, you can express it in your everyday life.

Journaling: a handmade life

In your journal, write about your experiences with clay. Have any of the images appeared in your daily life? Have your clay-making experiences spilled over into everyday life, perceptions, insights, behavior, self-image?

> Often the hands know
> how to solve a riddle that
> the mind has wrestled with in vain.
>
> —CARL JUNG

6. THE SOUND OF FEELINGS: FROM SADNESS TO JOY

You have already seen how emotions reveal themselves in matter: color, shape, line, and texture. You've also gotten in touch with feelings through clay. Now we'll explore a new medium: sound and music, the swirling soup of auditory vibrations that surrounds us. This chapter takes you further into the senses as you listen to the sound of feelings. In order to really hear our emotions, and our innermost selves, we will engage in creative listening, sound making, and musical play. Some of these activities will include expressing music through art.

Emotions and sound

The emotional impact of both sound and music is obvious. Lullabies are used to soothe babies to sleep, dance music gets people on their feet, serenades put us in a romantic mood. Ambient sound can also trigger emotions. Jackhammers irritate us, sirens startle and alarm us, the sound of a babbling brook relaxes us. Read the following list of familiar sounds. As you listen to each one with the inner ear of your imagination, observe your physical and emotional reaction.

- wind in the trees
- nails being pounded into wood
- birds warbling
- a loud fax tone beeping in your ear
- a cat purring
- car brakes screeching
- rain on the roof or windows
- an ambulance siren
- waves coming in and out on the shore

Did your body contract at the mere thought of any of these sounds? Which ones were relaxing? Did any of them trigger feelings of fear, anger, irritation, sadness? What about joy, love, or peace? When thinking of these sounds, did you see any mental pictures?

Sound as environment

We float in sound all the time. It is everywhere. Sound vibrations permeate our every pore. It is not just our ears that hear; our whole body does. This was shown in the play and movie *Children of a Lesser God,* which featured a moving portrayal of deaf young-sters "hearing" through physical vibrations. They were able to dance and sing by res-onating with the sound vibration, feeling it through their hands and bodies.

We come from a sound environment. In his book *The Secret Life of the Unborn Child,* Dr. Thomas Verny discusses the sounds that surround the developing human. The womb is no silent chamber. The fetus responds to the mother's heartbeat, and it listens actively from week twenty-four on. Research shows that after birth, a baby rec-ognizes its mother's voice, and it also reacts to music played while it was in utero.

Sound can contribute to our emotional and physical well-being, or it can cause stress. As far back as the 1970s, it was shown that rock music had a damaging effect on plant life whereas Baroque music enhanced the growth of our green friends. Responses to sound are very personal, as is taste in music. When we perceive a sound as disrup-tive, we refer to it as noise. One man's music may be another man's nuisance. "Turn that racket down!" the father calls to his teenage son. "You call that music?"

After some research, our society has officially accepted the fact that certain noises and sound levels can be hazardous to our health. Coining the term noise pollution, we have regulated sound in the public arena, especially in cities and factories where louder and louder equipment and vehicles are being used. In some communities, leaf blowers have been banned because of the racket they make. And it has now been shown that a habit of listening to amped-up music can result in hearing loss.

Music as medicine

Of all the sounds in the environment, what we call music stands out as a special cate-gory. Throughout the ages, music has been used universally to express feelings as well as to influence the emotions of others. Music (of our own making or someone else's) can be a powerful way to draw out feelings. As emotions come to the surface, we ex-perience them more fully and can accept them. A middle-aged business professional named Rob told me about how music on his car radio touched and healed some deeply buried grief. Right after the breakup of his fifteen-year marriage, Rob was driving on a long business trip. Suddenly the voice of Phil Collins came on the radio singing "Separate Lives." "He was singing about me," Rob told me. "The melody and words captured my feelings so perfectly. Someone else knew how I felt. It was as if Collins were sitting in the passenger seat, listening to my thoughts and echoing them back to me, the way a friend does."

Busy surviving and coping with daily life, Rob hadn't let himself feel the full pain of the separation. As the music drew out his emotions, tears started blurring his vision, forcing him to pull over to the side of the road for a good cry. Rob said he felt greatly relieved afterward and that this catharsis helped him through the weeks to come, during which the divorce became final. He allowed himself more quiet time alone, started keeping a feelings journal, and got in touch with emotions he'd never known he had. Rob also opened himself to opportunities and growth that came with his new situation.

Have you ever had an experience like Rob's? A piece of music presented itself at exactly the right moment; a song put into words something you hadn't been able to express but were feeling inside. Roberta Flack even recorded a song about this phenomenon, "Killing Me Softly," in which she says it was as if the singer had found her letters and was reading them out loud.

How can that happen? How is it that a total stranger can express our feelings for us? It's because music, poetry, and all the arts come from that subterranean ocean of the collective unconscious, the heart of the world. This common ground of emotions goes beyond space and time, transcends culture and beliefs. Emotions are the stuff that the universal human experience is made of. Feelings make us human and unite us with common threads. That is why, as the artist expresses his feelings, they resound in us, touching on emotional experiences we all have in one way or another.

Do you turn to music when you have strong or difficult emotions? What kinds of music do you associate with sadness? Happiness? Anger? Confusion? Music is certainly emotion in motion. Interestingly, in classical music, different segments of a piece are referred to as movements.

Music affects us physically, emotionally, mentally, and spiritually. Music can entertain, but it can also heal. Music is great medicine.

The feelings evoked by music, the experience of the rhythm, can be translated into lines, shapes, colors, and textures. Many people dance to music, but few draw or paint using sound to direct their movements. This activity series will enable you to do just that. It is like dancing on paper. The secret is to let the music flow through your body and out through your hands onto the paper.

MOOD MUSIC

Materials

Art paper, and drawing materials of your choice (chalk pastels, large felt markers, crayons, watercolors), recorded music of your choice

Activity

1. Play a piece of music that expresses your current feelings or an emotion you'd like to explore. Stand in front of your art paper and allow your body to sway or move to the music. Feel the music in your body.

2. With your *nondominant hand,* begin drawing or painting, using colors that express the emotion being evoked by the music. Let the movement of your hands and arms and your selection of color be guided by what you are hearing and feeling in your body. Feel the different instruments or voices in the music. What color, texture, shapes, and line quality does each one evoke?

   Do this as long as you wish. If you sense a need to change musical selections and work on a new piece of paper, feel free to do so. Do as many drawings or paintings to music as you like. You may want to experiment with using both hands simultaneously or alternately. For instance, one hand for the drumbeat and another for the flute (see the drawing on page 135).

3. Write about your experience in your journal, using your *dominant hand.*

Journal entry

I had been feeling very tense and out of sorts for about a week. My computer crashed and was in for repair. We still don't know what the problem is. I had been worried about whether I would meet my job deadline. If I don't deliver the work, I don't get paid. At the same time, I had some big financial setbacks last week: clients late with payments. I had been feeling very depressed about that.

At a workshop, I started drawing to the music that was being played. It could not have been more perfect. It began with a melancholy dirge that really captured my depression and disappointment. I did a pastel drawing in shades of gray—from dark charcoal to a milky light tone. There was also a lot of dark blue.

As the music shifted, a woman's solo voice was added to the orchestra. My mood shifted to the anxiety and even panic I had been feeling about the work deadline. I changed to another piece of paper and used black and bright red. It felt like waves in a stormy sea, and the strokes became more intense and animated. They had more energy. They weren't all tangled up the way the first drawing had been.

The third drawing was calmer, like a summer sea. Yet it had more freedom than when I began. The bottom half was done in the same black and bright red, and the top part was bright red with a little water added for blending into a pink sky area.

From listening, moving, and drawing out the feelings, my body got energized. I felt that I was taking back my power, instead of feeling so helpless, as I had all week.

The day after the workshop, I returned to work with a can-do attitude. I've been feeling much better—both physically and emotionally—since doing the drawings to music. The computer is still being repaired, but I got some help and will probably make my deadline. The financial problems are still there, but I am not obsessing about them. I'm taking things one day at a time. What a relief it was to get those feelings out of my system instead of carrying them around in my head and body.

Music as therapy

From the examples above, you can see the therapeutic nature of music. It can help liberate buried feelings and open up new levels of strength and creativity. Music therapy for mental and physical illness was one of the first modalities of expressive arts to be organized into a profession. In the past few decades music has been used for healing in hospitals, psychiatric and rehabilitation clinics, and educational institutions. Music as therapy actually goes back even further than that. It was used by a contemporary of Freud's named Georg Groddeck, author of *The Book of the It*. The two men corresponded, and Groddeck, who could probably be considered the father of modern holistic body-mind medicine, offered treatments at his healing spa to Freud, who was suffering with cancer. However, Freud declined.

I first heard about Groddeck's pioneering work, which included physical laying on of hands and psychotherapy, from an elderly chiropractor and practitioner of Chinese medicine, Dr. Ursula Greville. Born in England around the turn of the last century, Greville recalled frequent visits with her parents to Groddeck's healing spa on the Continent. From childhood, she had been gifted with an amazing voice and performed on the stage. At fifteen she sang the role of Queen of the Night in the Mozart opera *The Magic Flute*. At his spa, Groddeck would station the young singer outside the window of his treatment room to serenade during his sessions, especially when he was working with really difficult cases. Afterward he would always tell her, "Ah, yes! You're a natural born healer." Groddeck's comments about being a natural born healer always upset the young girl, who thought her future was in music. "No, I'm not a healer," she would object, "I hate sick people and I hate illness. Don't say that anymore." Groddeck turned out to be right. In later life Greville became a practitioner of several healing arts, including herbal medicine, and she strongly recommended music for inner balance.

As for the status of music as medicine today, this type of therapy has been widely documented and recently popularized by Don Campbell in his book *The Mozart Effect.* From the author's own fantastic story of self-healing (he shrank a dangerous blood clot in his brain) through his many case studies, this book carries the reader along on a magical ride. The sections that describe the groundbreaking work of French physician Dr. Alfred Tomatis and his miraculous results using the music of Mozart are especially inspiring. There are now Tomatis centers all over the world. Campbell also sites research such as the studies done at St. Agnes Hospital's critical care unit in Baltimore. For example, half an hour of music produced the same calming effect as ten milligrams of Valium.

Campbell has also made Mozart's music easily accessible in his compilation of three audiotapes entitled *Music for the Mozart Effect:*

- *Volume I, Strength of Mind* (to improve intelligence and learning)
- *Volume II, Heal the Body* (to promote rest and relaxation)
- *Volume III, Unlock the Creative Spirit* (to stimulate creativity and imagination)

I recommend these tapes for exploring the Mozart effect firsthand. The third volume is especially good for doing Inner Child work. It features the great composer's variations on an old folk song (sung in nursery schools and kindergarten as "Twinkle, Twinkle, Little Star" or the "ABC Song"). The playful and creative Inner Child comes alive to this music.

In addition to Campbell's work, I also recommend *The Tao of Music: Sound Psychology* by musician and psychologist Dr. John M. Ortiz. A practical guide to the transformative nature of music, it is filled with wonderful exercises and insights as well as case histories. Julia Cameron's book *The Vein of Gold: A Journey to Your Creative Heart* is also worth exploring. The chapter titled "The Kingdom of Sound" has many imaginative and playful exercises for experimenting with sound and music.

Another highly informative book that includes a discussion of music for healing is Susan Skog's *Depression: What Your Body's Trying to Tell You.* This practical guide to alternative treatment for depression also includes information about art therapy and writing therapy. This is a valuable book for anyone dealing with depression.

I'll be suggesting musical selections I use in workshops. They reflect a broad range of styles: jazz, classical, spiritual chants and hymns, vocal and instrumental music, and indigenous world music. I highly recommend *The Sound of Feelings,* the series created to go with this book, by Jessie Allen Cooper (see the Resources section).

Sounds around us

Certain sounds can stress us out, cause irritability and fatigue, and even impair our ability to think clearly. "I can't hear myself think," the victim of noise pollution cries. On the other hand, some sounds and certain musical expression can soothe, energize, or inspire. "Let's put on some mood music," a man says to his lover.

As mentioned earlier, we live in a sound environment. Some sounds are in our conscious awareness, some get blocked out. Like changing the focus on a camera lens or binoculars, we selectively tune in to different sounds while relegating others to a background blur. We turn up the volume in our inner ear to listen to what we choose to hear, and our sound focus can move around at any time. Listen for yourself. Try this sound meditation that I use for getting workshop participants centered in the present moment. Practice this when you want to relax. It is also great for discovering the effect that sound has on your emotions, your body, and your mental state.

Once you become fully aware of the impact sound has on you and on your emo-

The Hear and Now: Near and Far

Read through the guidelines, then do the activity with your eyes closed.

Listen to the sounds around you at this moment, starting with the ones closest to you. Close your eyes in order to isolate the sense of hearing. Tune in to the sounds of your own body. Can you hear your breathing? Your movements?

Let the first sounds you heard recede into the background of your awareness, turn up the inner volume on sounds a little farther away. Tune in to sounds in the room or space immediately around you. What do you hear? People, pets, machines, music, nature?

Continue this process by expanding your ears' reach even farther. What do you hear coming from adjoining spaces, rooms, buildings?

Shift your attention next to sounds that are even farther away: the neighborhood or territory within yards or blocks of where you are. What do you hear? A dog barking? A car driving past? Keep widening the circle of your hearing. What is the farthest sound you can hear? A siren several blocks away? An airplane overhead? Focus on each sound one at a time.

Then return to your own breathing and the rhythm of your heartbeat.

tions, it becomes possible to make choices. A good example is Noreen, a gifted pianist and retired music teacher. She began suffering from stress but couldn't figure out the cause. "I just feel irritable all the time and worn out," she told me. "I've been to the doctor and they couldn't find anything. It isn't anything in particular, like a difficult person or situation. I can't quite put my finger on it."

After a week's vacation in a remote mountain resort, Noreen realized what her problem was. Upon returning home, she discovered she could no longer tolerate the sounds of the city she lived in. The population and traffic had grown insufferably dense in the past couple of years, and the auditory landscape was filled with the sounds of traffic, car alarms, sirens, barking dogs, planes and helicopters from a nearby airport that had expanded. She decided to move to a smaller town in the country. Once there, her chronic irritability disappeared, and Noreen regained her health and peace of mind. "But, of course, I'm a musician. I love *beautiful* sound. Now I'm surrounded by nature—birds, a brook nearby, and blessed silence, especially at night. I sleep better than I have in years. And when I play the piano, I can really hear my music without all the background noise of the city."

Drumming and the hot emotions

Drumming is a wonderful way to express the hot emotions discussed in Chapters Four and Five, such as anger, passion, and sexuality. Drumming or playing any percussion instrument naturally evokes the kind of movement pattern that liberates these feelings. You don't need any training or talent in music to engage in percussive sound. And you don't even need bona fide musical instruments. Many common objects that we discard every day can be used as drums and percussion devices: oatmeal boxes, large ice cream containers, corrugated boxes, and plastic buckets. Wooden mixing spoons and sticks can be used as drumsticks, mallets, and rhythm clappers. The kitchen is a great place to look for musical instruments in disguise. That's why toddlers love to hang out on the kitchen floor and play with pots and pans and anything else they can get their hands on.

If you decide you like drumming and percussion, you might want to consider buying yourself a drum. This need not be expensive, and you might find one in the most unexpected places. Just set the intention and see what happens. After looking for just the right drum in music stores for several months, I had almost given up. Then while browsing around for home furnishings in a Pier One Imports store, I came across a display of large drums from Guinea. Each one sounded and felt different. After trying them all, I found the one. To me, there was something special about its particular tone and the way it felt when I hit it. Use your instincts and sense of touch and hearing to size up a drum. When you find the right one, you'll recognize it. My friends have found drums in street bazaars, import stores, art fairs, bookstores, Native American shops, and other specialty stores that sell crystals and other shamanic materials.

If you take to drumming, a must-read book is *Drumming on the Edge of Magic: A Journey into the Spirit of Percussion* by Mickey Hart, former Grateful Dead percussionist, and Jay Stevens. Part autobiography and part research into the history and lore of drumming and shamanic traditions, this book is a delightful and inspiring adventure. You also might want to check out his albums of world music and percussion.

Before doing the next activity, you might want to review the section on the hot emotions in Chapter Four.

Hot Sounds

Experiment with expressing the hot emotions of anger, passion, and sexuality with a drum or drumlike object. Close your eyes and really listen to the sounds you make. Experiment with using different parts of your hands. Vary the tempo and volume. Let the feelings come out into the drum, the way they did with art and with clay. Experiment with other percussive materials like sticks, wood blocks, rattles, etc.

Note: If you have access to a piano, try improvising your feelings on it. You don't need any training or special talent to do this. Just allow yourself to explore certain emotions on the instrument.

If you already play an instrument, try letting out your feelings through improvisation. And, of course, you can always use music you already know that expresses your current mood or emotion.

I recommend *The Sound of Feelings* CDs by Jessie Allen Cooper (see Resources). You can use the "Anger" side for drumming. I'd also like to recommend "Angry Man," a song written and performed by Bobby McFerrin on the album entitled *Medicine Music.* You'll be doing some dancing to it later on, but it is also great for listening. It really captures the emotion of anger in a creative way, a wonderful example of turning feelings into art. I strongly recommend that you get a tape or CD of *Medicine Music.* It contains many songs we'll be using at the end of this chapter and in the next.

Emotions and vocal sound

In addition to musical and other environmental sounds that evoke feelings, we also hear human vocal sounds that convey emotions. Speech and vocal utterances like a scream or laugh are used to communicate the whole range of human feelings. Vocal sound that is charged with emotion moves us. Someone yelling "Fire!" can get us out of a room in a flash. It's not the word so much as the tone of voice and the urgency in the voice. We don't need to see the person. If we sense that he or she is for real, we will vacate the place immediately and ask questions later. If the word "fire" had been delivered in a flat monotone completely devoid of affect (emotional oomph), our response would be quite blasé. We wouldn't take it seriously. It's the *way* the word is said, not just the word itself.

There are centers in the right hemisphere of the brain that govern this kind of emotionally charged vocal expression. The words may be associated with the left-hemisphere language centers, but the tone, inflection, and nuance of feeling are made possible by the emotionally expressive areas of the right hemisphere. Those who have had injuries or disease in this area are incapable of expressing emotions in speech. Likewise, individuals who have shut down their feelings owing to early trauma or who are temporarily in a state of shock are disconnected from this area of the brain. As a result, they speak in an emotionless monotone. When the right brain is working, we put feeling into our words. Then our emotion-filled vocal expressions also touch others.

Reflect on how you respond when you think of the following vocal sounds:

- a mother crooning a lullaby to her infant
- your lover whispering sweet nothings in your ear
- a man screaming "Thief, thief!"
- children laughing in a playground
- a toddler crying because it has fallen down
- a sportscaster excitedly describing a play

Vocalizing our feelings

To vocalize our pleasure as well as our pain is as natural as breathing. We hum, groan, moan, cry, sob, yell, scream, laugh, and giggle. We make these sounds automatically, without thinking. The feeling inside simply moves outward—emotions in motion—through our sound.

Our voice is like a fingerprint: it bears our stamp. That is why they use voice prints in forensic work. The way we use this wonderful gift is an expression of who we are. Our voice changes every day and every minute, reflecting our shifting moods and feelings. Levels of tension and relaxation, happiness and depression all show up in the tone, volume, and pitch of your voice. For example, many who practice massage therapy and bodywork have told me that people's voices usually become lower and more resonant after a massage. The body is relaxed and the voice follows suit.

Our change of voice is often more easily heard by others who listen to us from outside. Yet we can become more aware of our own voices as vehicles of our innermost feelings. Just as we used the visual arts for recognizing and releasing our emotions, we also can use our voice. But first we have to find our voice.

One of the great voice teachers of our time is Arthur Joseph. His list of clients and students sounds like the *Who's Who* of the entertainment and sports worlds. It has been my pleasure to study with Arthur and also to teach personal presentation classes with him at The Walt Disney Company. One of his tenets is that your voice has the power to instantly reach out and connect you with other people. Your voice also connects you with yourself. In his method, called Vocal Awareness, Arthur teaches the connection of voice to the soul, the spirit, and to feelings. If you really want to explore the power of the voice, consider getting Arthur's book, *The Sound of the Soul* or, better yet, use his audiotape programs, *Vocal Awareness* and *Sing Your Heart Out.* His videotape, *Vocal Awareness,* is also excellent. What comes through loud and clear in Arthur's approach is that when we finally find our true voice, it is love expressing through us or, as he puts it, the sound of the soul.

You'll be doing some vocal play in order to explore the range of expression possible with your voice. Before you begin, let me address the fear that often comes up for people when they are asked to make spontaneous vocal sound. As with art, they are afraid they will make a mistake, create ugly sounds, or be judged. I suspect that is why people sing in the privacy of the shower, but not outside it.

Let me repeat: There is no right or wrong way to do these vocal activities or any others in this book. Make it safe to do this work. If you need solitude, find it—in the bathroom, on a mountaintop, wherever you feel comfortable sounding your own feelings. Take the same precautions you did with your creative experiments in art. Don't do this activity around people who are critical of you. And do your best to relax and have fun with it. If your Inner Music Critic jumps out, ask it to wait until you are finished. You may even want to do the journal dialogue from Chapter Two.

Since voice depends on breath, we'll begin with a breathing meditation. Then we'll move into toning to relax and energize the body, followed by sounds for expressing emotions.

FINDING MY VOICE

Activity

1. Sit in a comfortable position and focus on your breathing. Place your hands just below your navel. Be aware of the rhythm of your breath coming in and going out. Allow the breath to become deeper and slower, filling your belly and whole body. Do this for a couple of minutes, letting yourself relax fully.

2. Now place your hands over your belly, locate the place where the power of your voice comes from, and follow it up and through your windpipe. Then as you exhale, start to let some sounds out. Any sound at all. Some suggestions are:

   - the whoosh of releasing the breath
   - a yawn
   - a sigh
   - an ah sound
   - a laugh
   - vowel sounds
   - a groan or moaning sound

3. Find a sound that you want to stay with for a while. Follow it where it takes you, experimenting with volume and pitch. You can do this as softly or loudly as you wish.

Sounding our depths: sadness, loneliness, and grief

In my therapy practice, I saw some dramatic transformations when clients could explore depression, sadness, loneliness, and grief through sound. These families of emotions are usually associated with low energy. However, by expressing them through sound, it is common to see a person's energy start to open and expand. Either on the piano or through vocal toning, these individuals were able to give voice to emotions that had been deeply buried or masked with a smile and an adult facade. The vulnerable and frightened Inner Child, who had been afraid to speak, often became quite expressive. Finding its voice, it had lots to say.

It takes a lot of energy to stuff our emotions and keep them in the closet. This is especially true for vulnerability and sadness, which are so often disowned in our over-civilized culture that prizes above all the relentless pursuit of happiness, power, and strength. Through vocal sounding and musical exploration, these emotions sometimes emerge in spontaneous song or chanted poetry. For those who play an instrument, these feelings may pour out on the piano, electronic keyboard, or guitar. There is an ancient instinctual urge to come out of ourselves through sound. When this natural ability is embraced, it brings about magical healing.

Heart Healing

I recommend revisiting the previous activities: "mood music" and "finding my voice." Focus on the emotions of sadness and loneliness. Perhaps other words like grief or depression come to mind. Allow the feeling to find a voice through your own sounds, vocal or otherwise.

Toning

Resonating the body with healing vowel sounds is called toning. It is an ancient practice used by shamanic healers around the world. But you don't have to be a healer, shaman, or medicine man to use toning on yourself.

Try making a vowel tone, and feel where it vibrates in your body. Use different pronunciations of the vowels: Ah, or a long A, E, I, O, Oo. Hold the tone for as long as you can. Do you feel a vibration in any part of your body? Do you feel it in your head? Your stomach? Your lower back? Sinus?

That is toning. It can be used to relax, heal, and energize body parts and internal organs. I was introduced to toning in the 1970s through the work of Laurel Elizabeth Keyes, author of *Toning: The Creative Power of the Voice*. I also studied with Chava Lassen, a vocal coach in Santa Monica, California, who worked with therapists, teachers, and others who used their voices in a therapeutic context. Chava's premise was that the tone and resonance of a person's voice communicated more than the content of his or her words. If therapists, physicians, nurses, and other healing professionals were going to influence their clients and patients toward health, they needed to be aware of their own voice and how it affected others. You can experiment with toning yourself. It's a great thing to do in the shower each morning, a good way to balance and energize yourself for the day.

Sounding the Body

If you are carrying any stress in a particular body part, experiment with making some vowel sounds. Find one that resonates with the area of your body that needs healing or energy. You'll actually feel the vibrations in that body part. It is a kind of dialogue between your inner self and whatever it is that is blocked in this particular body part.

Repeat these tones, sustaining them for as long as you can. The sound flies on the wings of your breath, so breathe deeply in order to produce a richer, more resonant sound. Afterward, see how your body feels.

Mantra and sound meditation: peace and contentment

One of the most ancient of spiritual practices is the chanting or silent recitation of a mantra. A mantra is a syllable, word, or phrase that is repeated over and over again. Widely used in Hinduism and other Eastern traditions such as Buddhism, the mantra is used as a focus to quiet the chattering mind. The word comes from the Sanskrit *manas* (mind) and *trai* (to protect, to free from). So a mantra helps free us from our mind, and it helps to protect us. Mantras are commonly used as an aid in meditation.

In the tradition I have studied, meditation is defined as the process through which one goes beyond the ego to experience the Inner Self, or one's divine essence. The goal is to experience the individual consciousness and universal consciousness as one. In sitting meditation, one finds a comfortable position and recites the mantra silently or out loud over and over. This sounds easy, but it isn't. Before the meditator realizes it, the mind wanders off to distracting thoughts like, "What dress am I going to wear to that party on Saturday night? Did I remember to pay the phone bill? Gee, my lower back really hurts." The chattering mind is like a gang of hyperactive children. It wants to do anything but stay in the here and now. When the meditator realizes that the mind has wandered, the focus of attention is pulled back to the mantra.

Mantra repetition can also be done throughout the day, turning any activity into a form of meditation. Anchoring us into the present moment, a mantra can provide a safe harbor in the storm of daily stresses and a life governed by the busy brain. A good book on meditation is Swami Muktananda's *Meditate*.

As a focus for the mind in meditation, a mantra can be as simple as one syllable, such as *Om* (considered the primal sound in Eastern spiritual practices). It can also be a word or phrase, like *Hari om,* or the Tibetan Buddhist chant *Om mane padme hum.* Mantras have meaning—like the ancient Sanskrit one I was taught, *Om Namah Shivaya,* which means, "I honor the God within." There are mantras that praise or simply say the name of God. When Gandhi was assassinated, he died with a mantra on his lips, God's name in Sanskrit, *Ram.*

In adapting mantra meditation, people from the West often repeat a short affirmation of prayer such as "I am blessed" or "Glory to God." Others use a short series of syllables that have no meaning at all. I personally prefer the ancient Sanskrit mantras because they are time-tested, sacred sounds invested with power to transform or protect the person who repeats them. They vibrate the body's energy centers, or chakras, and clear the body-mind and strengthen the spiritual energy field. My favorite mantra tape is *The Power of the Mantra* with Gurumayi Chidvilasanada. For more history and information about mantras, you may want to get Thomas Ashley-Farrand's cassette series, *Mantra: Sacred Words of Power.*

Mantra Meditation

Create your own mantra or find one that suits you, using the suggestions given above. Remember, this is a syllable or series of syllables that you repeat.

Spend a few minutes each day reciting or chanting your mantra. You can do this in sitting meditation, in the shower, while driving the car, walking in nature, or any other place where you feel comfortable.

If you find yourself getting confused or scattered throughout the day, or obsessed with worries, remember to repeat your mantra silently in your mind.

A meditative atmosphere

There are some wonderful tapes and CDs available that feature meditative music and sound. These can be used simply for listening or for accompanying art activities from the previous two chapters. They also can be used for meditative movement and dance, which we'll explore in the next chapter. You may have some recorded music of your own that is suitable for creating a meditative environment through sound. Here are some of my favorite tapes and CDs for meditation:

Canyon Trilogy and *Inner Voices,* Native American flute music by R. Carlos Nakai
Hildegard von Bingen: Symphoniae by Sequentia Ensemble for Medieval Music
Light from Assisi by Richard Shulman
Medicine Music by Bobby McFerrin ("The 23rd Psalm," "Common Threads")
Music for Zen Meditation and Other Joys, Clarinet, Koto and Shakuhachi played by
     Tony Scott, Shinchi Yuze, and Hozen Yamamoto
Nature's Chant, Gregorian chant and nature sounds from NorthSound
Sunlit Reverie, flute music by Radhika Miller
Transformation at Assisi by Richard Shulman

Sounds from the heart: happiness, love, and playfulness

Music is one of the most common ways to express the joyful emotions. Through song and instrumental music, sometimes accompanied by dance, humans have awakened the effervescence of their own inner happiness. "Make a joyful sound unto the Lord," the Bible exhorts us. Whether praising God in gospel hymns or crooning a love song, the musician and singer reach to the heights of human delight. Beyond peace and contentment, we move into bliss.

Interestingly, we use the term *play* to describe the musician's engagement with his instrument. From a jazz combo to a symphony orchestra, the members of the group *play* their music. This is no accident, for it is the playful Child Within who carries us beyond the ego, into the realm of pure enchantment. The heart opens and magical sound pours out, taking us in flight. Look through your own collection for music that expresses these emotions. Jessie Allen Cooper's music has always evoked feelings of playfulness, joy, and freedom when I've used it in workshops.

Bobby McFerrin's *Medicine Music* contains several pieces for exploring happiness, joy, and love. We'll encounter it again in the next chapter when we discover the Dancer Within. The songs that epitomize happiness, love, and playfulness are:

"Medicine Man" (happiness)
"Baby" (playfulness and love)
"Yes, You" (love)
"Soma so de la de sase" (playfulness)
"Common Threads" (love)
"Sweet in the Mornin'" *(love)*
"The 23rd Psalm" (love, joy)

Activities

Revisit art activities in Chapters Four and Five and do the ones of your choice again. This time play recorded music while engaged in art making. Let the rhythms and melodies direct your movements as you work with the materials. Experiment with closing your eyes, using your *nondominant hand,* and also using both hands.

Music for exploring the sound of feelings

In closing this chapter, I'll say a little more about the music of my dear friend Jessie Allen Cooper. Jessie is an established recording artist, performer, and visual artist.

When I told this multitalented friend that I was writing this book, he and I revived an old dream we had shared: to create music to accompany my expressive arts work.

Jessie has created a series of musical accompaniments for the nine Families of Feelings listed in the beginning of this book. His set of recorded music is called *The Sound of Feelings*. The first selection features my narration introducing the concept of using music and sound as a gateway into our emotions and also a vehicle for expressing them in combination with the other art forms. The other nine parts of this ten-segment series are devoted to the families of feelings. Jessie's music can provide you with a complete set of accompaniments for all the activities in this book—for drawing, painting, sounding, or dancing your feelings out, or just listening to the sound of feelings. *The Sound of Feelings* series is especially suited as a musical soundtrack for the movement and dance activities in the next chapter. It is available at coopersoundwaves.com.

7. EMOTIONS IN MOTION: MOVING YOUR MOOD, DANCING FOR JOY

Body language and emotions

We have already explored how emotions get unconsciously lodged in body parts. In Chapter Three we used art and writing to liberate imprisoned feelings. That was a good beginning, but the feelings in our body want more. They want to *move*. They want to be physically playful and experimental the way we were as kids. Our feelings want to *dance*.

In order to do the activities in this chapter, you will need a small floor space in which you can move spontaneously. How large your movements get will be determined by how much space you have. In warm weather it can even be an outdoor area.

Other materials needed
   Sound system
   Your collection of recorded music

Audiotapes of Gabrielle Roth
   Endless Wave
   Initiation
   Trance
   Ordering information is in the Resources section under Roth, Gabrielle.

Also recommended: *The Sound of Feelings* series by Jessie Allen Cooper
   (See Resources for information about all the music listed.)

The Dancer Within

When I think of dance and childhood, I recall feeling a deep longing. In my early years, like so many little girls, I wanted nothing more than to be a dancer. I pleaded with my parents for ballet lessons, but to no avail. Although they were completely supportive of the arts, my parents were concerned about my health. I had been diagnosed with a slight heart murmur, so ballet class was out of the question. My natural talents and love of music were channeled into piano and organ lessons and singing in a Gregorian chant choir, but the dancer in me was always gnawing away in my soul.

It was the retrieval of this Dancer Within that really inspired me to write this book. I know how torturously difficult it is for people to express themselves in the arts when they believe they can't or shouldn't. I grew up thinking that if I danced I might die. Images of heart attacks hovered in my brain. It was like the forbidden apple in the Garden of Eden. What a dilemma: fearing the very thing you most desire. Things changed somewhat in adolescence, of course. I participated in ballroom dancing at sock hops and proms, but this was a very prescribed form of dance: there were steps and movements to learn. I hadn't discovered the inner dance of unique, spontaneous expression.

Then at age thirty-nine something snapped in me. After healing myself through art and writing and changing careers, the Inner Dancer started screaming. With the discovery of the Inner Child came the realization that this dancer had been locked up all my life. No longer would she be silent and immobilized. There was nothing left to do but let her out. I couldn't get enough movement classes, weekend workshops, and dance therapy institutes. At my first workshop with dance therapist Joan Chodorow, I ended up weeping. Moving around the floor with a newfound freedom, all I could do was cry—for what I had lost and for what I had found.

Fortunately, I had access to a succession of truly inspiring teachers of movement in the Los Angeles area. I am eternally indebted to them for helping me let the Inner Dancer out of the closet. They did for me what I am attempting to do for you: to show you how to lay aside your apprehension and fear, to revive the artist that waits inside. Is it your visual artist, your musician or composer, your storyteller or actor that has been silenced? Is it your dancer that has been squelched? It may be one or more of the above.

Throughout this chapter, I'll be drawing on the inspiration and methods of my teachers, movement pioneers like:

- Emilie Conrad, who developed the Continuum method
- Gabrielle Roth, whose audio programs we'll be using in this chapter
- Ruth Gould Goodman, healer and teacher extraordinaire
- Mariane Athey Karou, creator of Dance Alive! and the best guide to Inner Child movement I know
- Katja Biesanz, whose class You Are a Dancer convinced me that I was
- Prema Devi, who taught me the Inner Dance
- John Jones, who taught me the joys of ballroom dancing as art and therapy

Their presence is with me as I write this chapter. So please join us in the search to find *your* Inner Dancer.

Blocks to spontaneous dance

Dance and movement bring up a lot of feelings—a whole lot. Dance also brings up blocks and resistance to free expression. For instance, workshop participants who are critical of their body size and shape are terrified of "parading" themselves on the dance floor, as one woman described it. I've been in that category, so I know how it feels. The Inner Critic says things like, "You're too fat or too thin or too tall or too short, you're too old for this." Something like that may be going on in your mind right now. "Oh, I'll just skip this chapter," you might be thinking.

People who were told they were clumsy and awkward as children, as I was, are also afraid of getting up and demonstrating their "oafishness," to use one man's term. They often say they have two left feet. All I ask is that you read the chapter and try the activities. There are no prescribed steps to learn and no technical standards being set. You will be doing these activities alone, away from the eyes of others who you fear might make fun of you.

Why can't we move and dance spontaneously the way children do? What gets in our way? The answer is simple: the same thing that keeps us from drawing or making music or writing or acting just for the fun of it. It's the Inner Critic again. We are afraid we'll make a mistake. And the way out of that dilemma is the same as in earlier chapters. There is no right or wrong way to do the activities. So how on earth can you make a mistake? Errors only happen when there is an expectation or level of performance being aspired to. That doesn't exist here, so please do your best to relax and travel with me to find your Inner Dancer.

I realize that the very word *dance* can be intimidating. One thinks of Arthur Murray and dance steps and "getting it right" and fear of making mistakes or being awkward. What we're doing here is different, not better or worse, just different.

Moving your feelings out

As with all the other activities in this book, in expressive dance the focus is on feelings first: finding and letting them out through movement. Spontaneous dance and move-ment are used primarily as a vehicle for emotions, not to entertain others. The key word here is *spontaneous*. You will not be directed in any particular style of movement. There are no dance steps to learn. Rather, you will be offered suggestions for reflecting feelings with and through your body, letting your emotions out into the world. At the same time, you will be looking inward to recognize and embrace your feelings.

You actually started this dance process when you did art with a music accompani-ment and when you played with rhythms on drums and percussion devices. Now you will use your whole body as the instrument through which your feelings flow. This sort of improvisational movement is really a form of meditation. It is intended to help you experience your body and emotions more fully in the present moment. The first move-ment activity will be done in silence. As you move in the silence, listen for your own Inner Music.

Interestingly, while preparing to write this section, I happened upon an interview with the great mime Marcel Marceau on a television news report. Marceau was asked where his movement comes from. His answer: The movement comes from feeling and musicality. He even mentioned that many musicians had asked him over the years if he hears music while performing. Having seen Marceau on the stage many, many years ago, I could understand this question. The fluidity and rhythm of Marceau's move-ments, done in total silence, are exquisite poetry and music embodied in the human form. Marceau said that he does hear an inner music while he mimes.

MOVEMENT MEDITATION

Materials

A large enough space in which to move freely. You'll need at least two arm's length of clear space all around you. Comfortable clothes (no shoes).

Avoid having any mirrors around. This will only invite your Inner Critic to come out and judge how you look. If you can't remove the mirrors, close your eyes or turn your back to them.

Note: If you are temporarily or permanently handicapped and cannot stand, do this activity and all the others seated in a comfortable position.

Activity

1. Stand in the center of a space you have designated as your "dance floor." If standing, place your feet parallel and hips'-width apart. Plant yourself on the ground like a tree, with your knees soft and flexible. Allow your arms to hang comfortably by your side. Imagine roots extending from the soles of your feet down deep into the earth.

2. Allow yourself to breathe evenly and rhythmically. On the inhale, notice how nurtured you are by the breath of life. On the exhale, allow the breath to carry away any tension in your body. Let it melt like ice and flow into the ground. Release and relax your body.

3. Listen quietly to your body and your emotions.

   - How do you feel physically right now?
   - How do you feel emotionally?

4. Slowly allow your body to adopt a posture that expresses how you feel—both physically and emotionally.

- What kind of body posture expresses how you feel? For instance, fear might move you into a protective, fetal position. Anger might evoke an emphatic stance. Love could express through widespread arms or an embracing gesture. Find your own form.

- Can you extend that simple gesture into movement that speaks for your feeling self? Follow the movement within and let it take you where it wants to go. Let your body lead you. It knows what it wants to say. Do this for a few minutes. As you move, see if you can get in touch with that life-force energy flowing through your body. It is called chi in Asian traditions and prana in India. You may feel it as heat or as a tingly sensation. Watch where it is traveling in your body.

5. When you are finished, stand or sit quietly for a moment.

This is a wonderful meditation to be practiced daily, the way people do warm-ups and stretches. It not only helps release stiffness and stress but gets you in touch with an energy force within yourself that literally has a mind of its own. If you let it, that inner energy will move you to new levels of awareness and aliveness.

The work of Gabrielle Roth and the five rhythms

Now we will explore the work of one of my movement mentors, Gabrielle Roth. I first met Roth at a dance therapist's conference in the mid-'70s, during the start of my art therapy career. This tall, lithe figure with long dark hair took the stage and led the large crowd of several hundred in group movement. We all went into a kind of meditative trance, lost in our bodies, in the moment and in the dance. It was mesmerizing. In a smaller group workshop that followed, she led us into our senses and intuition through interactive exercises done in pairs. The experience convinced me to include movement in my private art therapy practice and workshops.

A dynamic workshop leader and author, Gabrielle has probably done more to get people up on their feet and dancing spontaneously than anyone on the planet. She travels worldwide, appearing at large conferences and smaller workshops where she invites the Inner Dancer out to play. I think of her as the Pied Piper of dance. She can get several hundred adults moving about on a ballroom floor like kindergartners. Although I haven't spent much time with Gabrielle and her musician husband and partner, Rob, I have been deeply influenced by their work. Their wonderful audiotapes and CDs serve as accompaniment for movement explorations in my own workshops. If you want to nurture your Inner Dancer, read Gabrielle's book, *Sweat Your Prayers*.

Gabrielle's work is distinguished by her exploration of what she calls the five rhythms: flowing, staccato, chaos, lyrical, and stillness. Moving to music that captures these five rhythms, one embodies the creative process itself. The key word here is *embody*. It's one thing to philosophize and talk about the creative process; it is another to feel it in your body. That is what Gabrielle helps us do. Each of the five basic rhythms evokes its own characteristic gestures, movement patterns, and emotional tone. The five rhythms parallel and embody the stages of the creative process.

The Five Rhythms and the Creative Process

FLOWING. This parallels the first stage of the creative process: getting your first inspiration, brainstorming, free associating, experimenting, researching, seeing the big picture. It often expresses in round and curved motions, is inclusive and open-ended.

STACCATO. This rhythm is evocative of the more focused, goal-oriented, and purposeful stage of the creative process. In workshops, I often see straight lines, jagged forms, and linear patterns being expressed in people's movement and drawings to this rhythm.

CHAOS. This is the heart of the creative process: the place where the paradigm shift occurs, the new order is emerging but hasn't revealed itself yet. This is also the most difficult point. Many walk away from a creative venture at this point. In workshops, some people even feel a little nauseated or confused during this rhythm. They may wander around, go around in circles in a jumble or in many directions in quick succession. In chaos, we often feel lost. If we go through it, we will be found.

LYRICAL. This is the stage in which, if we surrender to the creative spirit, we find our true expression. The dance dances us, the painting paints itself, the song sings through us. We become the hollow reed through which the divine wind blows. This is where the new form emerges.

STILLNESS. Finally we reach the biblical seventh day on which God rested. We silently hold the creative process that has happened, contemplating the spirit that has been birthed through us. We feel the grace and the fullness of emptiness of which many spiritual teachers have spoken.

The Five Rhythms and Emotional States

When I started using Gabrielle's audiotapes to accompany movement in my workshops, it soon became clear that the five rhythms did more than just embody the creative process. They also created a sound environment within which to feel and dance emotions. I saw how similar this was to the activities of scribbling and drawing to music that I had been teaching.

As my students moved through the five rhythms, a whole host of emotions naturally came tumbling out. This was especially true when people started moving to the staccato rhythm. This rhythm seemed to give them permission to stomp angrily around the floor, punch the air, elbow their way in mock aggressiveness through space. They played with emotional energy as just that: pure energy. They weren't mad at anyone in the room. They didn't get into any actual fistfights. They were just dancing out their generalized and accumulated anger, getting it off their chest through full-body movement. And what relief they felt! And they felt playful, too.

Some of the workshop participants who strongly resisted doing the movement activities ended up loving them the most. They especially enjoyed doing an angry dance to the staccato rhythm and they learned to accept feelings of confusion and even the panic of not knowing as they danced the chaos rhythm. Many adults who come to my workshops are going through big life transitions: divorce, job loss, career change, and relocation. Feelings of chaos, turbulence, and confusion are a big part of their lives. Moving through the five rhythms helps them cope with these emotions creatively and lets them put chaos into context. It is a necessary part of life and the creative process, but only one phase.

We will be working with Gabrielle's five rhythms in the next set of activities. You can use selections from your own music collection as an alternative, but it's much easier to use her tapes or CDs because the rhythms are all there in sequence.

THE RHYTHMS OF FEELING

Materials

Floor space, sound system, and Gabrielle Roth's audiotape or CD *Endless Wave, Volume One* (or recorded music from your collection that contains selections using the five rhythms), journal, and felt pens

Activity

1. Put on side one of *Endless Wave, Volume One.* It's called "The Wave I."
2. Follow Gabrielle's voice through the body part warm-up at the beginning. She will lead you through your body from head to toe.
3. Continue listening and moving to the audio as Gabrielle guides you in moving to the five rhythms.
4. When track one ends, take a little break. Then play the next track. Move to the five rhythms again, and this time be aware of any emotions that come up.

   • Do you feel any particular emotion or family of feelings being expressed in the music?

- Does your mood change as the rhythms do?
- How is the change of rhythms and moods reflected in your movement?

5. When you feel finished, close your eyes and stand or sit quietly in silence. Experience the subtle movement inside your body.
6. Sit comfortably with your journal. Using your *nondominant hand,* write about your experience with the five rhythms. You can draw your impressions as well.

- What was it like to move through the five rhythms?
- Were any rhythms difficult for you?
- Did you enjoy any particular one more than the others?
- Did any of the rhythms evoke strong emotions?
- Draw or write out your reflections in your journal.

Next we will explore Gabrielle's five rhythms through a warm-up dance, followed by drawing to the rhythms. You can use the *Endless Wave* audio for this.

DRAWING THE FIVE RHYTHMS

Materials

Floor space, sound system, and audio of Gabrielle Roth's *Endless Wave, Volume One,* crayons or pastels, five pieces of art paper, journal, and felt pens.

Activity

1. Put on side one of *Endless Wave, Volume One.*
2. As you did in the last activity, follow Gabrielle's voice through the body parts warm-up and the five rhythms movement.
3. When side one is finished, turn on side two. This time, draw to the five rhythms using *either or both hands at once.* Do one drawing for each of the rhythms. Be

Drawing the Five Rhythms

aware of your movements as you draw. Observe the colors you choose and the textures and lines that spontaneously flow from the music.

4. If any feeling words come to mind as you draw each rhythm, write it into your drawing with your *nondominant hand.*

Once you know what they are, you may want to find each of the five rhythms in your own collection of recorded music. Experiment with dancing first and drawing later.

Trance dancing: when the spirit moves you

My favorite dictionary definition for *trance* is "a state of mystical absorption." In trance dancing your movement is improvised and spontaneous—anything goes. Follow your instincts and intuition as you allow the music to move through you.

You will know you have arrived at the state when you lose all sense of time and place and immerse yourself in the sound vibrations that are moving through your body. Immersing yourself in rhythm and mood, you eventually become one with the music and the dance. This may not happen at first. It may take time to relax into your own free-form dance. The Inner Critic will want to stand aside and make comments, judging and analyzing. Or the chattering mind will start digressing with thoughts about the past and the future—anything to avoid the here and now. When that happens, just become aware of it and return your awareness to the music and back into your body. The music is your mantra. The dance is your moving meditation.

I recommend using Jessie Allen Cooper's music, *The Sound of Feelings,* or music from your own collection. It is advisable to select longer instrumental pieces, perhaps a half hour long, so that you have time to surrender to the music. For that purpose, Cooper's series is perfect because each side is devoted to a different emotion. This gives you an opportunity to experience a particular feeling in depth. Use your whole body as the medium of expression, the instrument, the raw material. When trance dancing, whatever your body wants to do is the right way to move. Let the spirit of the music move you. Eventually you may experience your body as a temple of the spirit.

If you can allow the music to shape your dance instead of your trying to fabricate the movements, it can literally wash away stress and tensions held in your body. Think of the music as a shower that is cleansing you both externally and internally. Let this particular combination of sounds and rhythms be reflected in your body. Music that moves you can wear through the old encrusted patterns of holding tension—like water wearing down rocks. It doesn't matter what your mood is: sad, fearful, angry, joyful, or peaceful. Remember Marceau's statement, "The movement comes from feeling and musicality."

MOVING THE MUSIC

Materials

Floor space, sound system, *The Sound of Feelings* music by Jessie Allen Cooper, or music from your own collection

Activity

1. Choose one of the nine families of feelings. Select music that expresses that feeling and play it on your sound system.
2. Listen to the music, then let the mood of the music move itself out through your body.

- Can you feel the emotions being expressed in the music?
- As you move for a while, does your mood change? If so, go with it.

Stay with the music that is playing or find another piece that captures your mood.

3. When you feel finished, stand or sit quietly in silence and experience the movement inside your body.

4. Sit comfortably with your journal. With your *nondominant hand,* write about your experience with the movement.

- How did you feel moving to the music? Could you surrender to it?
- Did you feel comfortable moving spontaneously, or was it difficult?
- Did any particularly strong emotions come up?

The inward emotions: sadness, vulnerability, and fear

Movement can be a powerful way to explore feelings of sadness, vulnerability, and fear. In the context of body movement, I call this family of feelings the inward emotions. My observation over the years is that people usually turn in on themselves when they create postures to express these emotions. The inward turning happens in two ways: The body actually curls in upon itself as if for protection and cradling, and one's energy gets pulled inward.

The first kind of inward movement is obvious because you can see and feel it as a physical gesture. The second form of inward turning is more subtle. Yet we experience it all the time. When people feel sick or are sad, fearful or depressed, we can usually tell the difference in their energy level. They are quieter, they move less and they talk less. We might say to someone in this state, "What's wrong? You're not yourself today." When the person has recovered from this low energy level, we often say, "I'm glad to see that you are your old self again."

This family of emotions can be explored specifically through earlier activities in this chapter. You can move in silence, as well as with music that matches your specific mood.

Revisit the earlier activities, "movement meditation" and "moving the music." Express this family of feelings—sadness, grief, vulnerability, depression, fear, and so on—through gesture and spontaneous postures. Then allow the expression to expand through movement and dance. As you do this, be aware of what your body is saying.

- How does your body feel?
- What does your body need?
- Is it asking for comfort, protection, rest?
- Does it need a nap, to be wrapped in a blanket?
- What emotions do you feel?
- What do your emotions want?

Revisit the art media you used in Chapters Four and Five.

- Draw, paint, or sculpt the emotion first.
- Gesture and then dance out the image in the artwork.
- Write your reflections in the journal using either hand.

Note: You can also reverse the order and do the movement first, followed by the artwork.

Nurturing the self: love and self-care

When you are in a mood to nurture yourself or if you feel the need for comfort, gestures and movement can be very soothing.

Revisit the earlier activities, "movement meditation" and "moving the music." I recommend two cuts from Bobby McFerrin's *Medicine Music* recording: "The 23rd Psalm" and "Common Threads."

Art can also be used to strengthen your feelings of tender loving care toward yourself. This can be done by making representational pictures (such as a face or person) as well as with scribbles and abstract drawing. Clay can also be a powerful medium when used after some movement activity. The art piece may then inspire a new dance.

Revisit the art media you used in Chapters Four and Five.

- Gesture and then dance the emotion.
- Draw, paint, or sculpt the emotion.
- Use the art piece as the inspiration for another dance or gesture.

Write your observations and insights in your journal using your dominant hand.

Taking a stand: protectiveness and assertiveness

Sometimes your vulnerable or frightened Inner Child may be asking you for protection. It wants you to *put your foot down* and *take a stand.* Try a silent, standing meditation.

Taking a Stand

Plant yourself firmly on the floor, standing tall like a tree. Imagine roots going down from your feet into the center of the earth. Feel your strength and resolve building as you take energy from the ground up through your roots. Use this posture to be there for your vulnerable Inner Child when needed.

Revisit the earlier activities, "movement meditation" and "moving the music." Focus on feelings of assertiveness, protectiveness, and strength. Find the word that best describes the feeling for you.

Follow your movement with a drawing or clay piece that portrays these feelings. It might even be a portrait of you taking care of yourself or your Inner Child.

If you wish, create a dance inspired by your art piece.

Reflect on your experience in the journal using whichever hand you like.

Outgoing feelings: anger, passion, and sexuality

In contrast to the inward-turning emotions we explored earlier, the hot emotions such as anger, passion, and sexuality appear to move outward. In movement activities with private clients or groups, I notice that the energy in the room invariably shifts. You can feel the heat in the atmosphere and the power of these emotions as they pour out into the space.

You have already expressed these emotions in art and with sound and music; now try expanding out into full-body movement. Afterward you may want to integrate all the art media you've learned so far: moving, drawing, sculpting, and making sound. Follow your own instincts on how to combine these media for yourself.

Revisit the earlier activities, "movement meditation" and "moving the music." If you use Gabrielle Roth's recordings, use the "staccato" rhythm for releasing anger, or use the "anger" side on *The Sound of Feelings* set.

Follow your dance with a crayon or oil pastel drawing or with a clay sculpture. Make vocal sounds while doing your artwork or use a music accompaniment. Think of art making as a continuation of your dance.

Movement as spiritual practice: peace and serenity

Movement is a sublime form of meditation and prayer. Dance and movement have been used all over the world as part of religious and spiritual rituals throughout history. We see various gestures and ritual postures in ancient Egyptian art and in sculptures and meditation banners from India and Tibet. In the East, hand gestures called mudras are a form of moving mantra done during meditation. Some of them are used intentionally, but often mudras come spontaneously as the spirit moves through the meditator's body. The most familiar mudras are seen on statues of the Buddha in gestures conveying blessing, compassion, peace, or protection.

For many indigenous people today, dance still plays a central role in their lives and in their spiritual practice. This is especially true in places like Bali and parts of Africa. Even cultures who were colonized to near extinction, like the Native Americans and the Australian Aborigines, have clung to the dance and ritual of their spiritual heritage.

Prayer Dance: Temple of the Spirit

Revisit the earlier activities, "movement meditation" and "moving the music." Focus on peace and tranquillity. I recommend R. Carlos Nakai's *Canyon Trilogy* or *Pianoscapes* by Michael Jones or "peace" on the *Sound of Music* series. "Amazing Grace" on Nakai's *Inner Voices* is lovely.

Create a prayer through dance. Bobby McFerrin's "23rd Psalm," on the *Medicine Music* album, is excellent for this. Another favorite of mine for prayer dance is a piece from the James Ingram album, *It's Your Night*. The cut is entitled "Yah Mo B There" and includes Michael McDonald's voice. You can also use Gregorian chant or other tapes suggested in Chapter Four for evoking and expressing feelings of peace and serenity.

Try combining media, dance first, and then work with art materials.

Dance and vocalize your feelings at the same time.

Explore writing your own prayer in the journal after you've done your movement meditation. Write the prayer with your nondominant hand.

Roots and wings: joy, playfulness, and creativity

When Western people think of dancing, they think almost exclusively of parties, celebrations, and nightclubs. Although dance has nearly disappeared from our churches and temples, it has survived in our homes and places of entertainment. I am not including professional dance performance here, because this book focuses on art making, not on the spectator. Just remember that most of us danced as children, and that as teenagers we used dance as part of our dating ritual, our way to meet and get to know potential partners.

Dance has survived as a way to celebrate life. And in that vein, we use it in expressive arts as a way to dance our joy. Even if we feel down when we begin, the very act of dancing often uplifts our hearts and spirits.

Free-form Movement: The Dance of Life

Express joy and happiness, creativity and enthusiasm through dance. Revisit the earlier activity, "moving the music." Choose some music that expresses these emotions for you.

As you did earlier, combine media by alternating between dance, sound, and working with art materials.

Dance while vocalizing your feelings. Let yourself laugh and make sounds that express joy.

With your nondominant hand, write a poem that expresses this family of feelings.

Emotions as energy

In exploring your feelings through dance, I hope you have had a firsthand experience of emotions as energy. There is no bad or good emotion. They are simply energies that pass through us. They can get stuck, like water in a clogged pipe, or they can flow freely. Movement and dance are wonderful and playful ways to allow these energies to be alive in you.

Sylvia Ashton-Warner, author and teacher of Maori children in New Zealand, used to speak of the "creative vent" for allowing children's anger, sadness, fears, and pain to come out safely. For Ashton-Warner the creative vent was the arts. Think of all the media you've experienced so far as an ever-expanding creative vent for all your emotions. Let these art forms be your mirror in which you see yourself from the inside out.

PART THREE

Understanding Your Feelings

Insight through words

When language is used to articulate creative expression, both sides of the brain meet and embrace each other. In expressive arts, it is true that the work begins with creating a picture, sculpture, music, dance, and so on from the right brain, but it doesn't stop there. Eventually the expressive artist uses words. Our emotions, insights, and deep inner guidance want a voice. As you've seen throughout this book, we have followed each arts exploration with verbal expression in the Creative Journal. The notion of the body as storyteller or of letting pictures talk is familiar by now. You have already translated nonverbal media experiences into words through journaling. Now you will turn to storytelling itself through poetry and prose. Then you will create masks and let them speak. Last comes the exploration of old beliefs and the creation of new ones. Here is where feelings and imagination join together, enabling you to live your passion.

8. WHEN YOUR FEELINGS TELL THEIR STORY, PAY ATTENTION

In our journey to embrace and express our feelings, we finally arrive at words. Although the expressive arts experience begins with nonverbal sensory images, sooner or later we cross the corpus callosum bridge, that bundle of nerve fibers that connects the right brain with the left. We enter the world of words in the left brain. A story unfolds in time and space. "First this happened and then that occurred and someone reacted and then acted (or failed to act) and then something else happened . . ." and so on. A character moves through life experience, responding, shaping, and being shaped by his or her environment. Now we are experiencing sequential events. We've crossed into the land of the left hemisphere: the domain of spoken and written language.

In the beginning was the Word

Storytelling is as old as human culture. In fact, it may be the glue that holds a group together. Narratives about the past not only re-create but also help to create anew the identity of nations, states, cities, neighborhoods, tribes, and families. Creation stories tell about who we are, where we came from, where we're going after death, and about our relationship to a higher or transcending power. All the great religions and spiritual paths rely on storytelling and prophecies to weave together their beliefs, teachings, and practices. Scriptural commentaries, sermons, and hymns are all intended to serve the living word of divine wisdom.

Stories are told in many shapes and forms: a mother soothing her sick child to sleep with a fairy tale, a black American preacher inspiring his congregation with a word-jazz riff on a Jesus story, a multimillion-dollar *Star Wars* episode in which professional storytellers hope to enthrall the masses with the primal conflict between forces of light and dark, good and evil.

What is common to all great storytelling, from homespun yarn to box-office bonanza, is that it speaks to the universal human condition. It moves us, touching deep feelings within our hearts and souls. We cheer with the heroic figures, hiss the villain, sit on the edge of our seats as the conflict unfolds and comes to a climax, and sigh in relief as the story comes to a resolution. If it is a quieter, more introspective tale, we still find ourselves in it, as we feel with the characters, identify with one or more of them, and get emotionally involved.

If we don't feel anything, the story has failed us. Perhaps it speaks to someone else, but not to us. When a tale does mirror our own experience, we say, "Yes, that's my story, too." It could be Romeo and Juliet reminding you of an ill-fated romance you had in high school, or Medea enacting the explosive emotions you felt during the turmoil of your own divorce. Perhaps it's a love story like the movie *When Harry Met Sally,* which may echo the ups and downs in your own relationship. These tales have the ring of personal truth because they resonate with what is common to all human experience. Stories tell us that we are all one at the deepest level of our being.

Whether it be in the form of scripture, parables, fables, historical accounts, or fiction, stories give us a glimpse of universal human predicaments. The individual storyteller is like a funnel through which a powerful force flows. C. G. Jung called it the collective unconscious—an underground ocean filled with symbols, myths, and characters called archetypes. Whether it is the giant in Jack and the Beanstalk or Darth Vader, the essence of that archetype is the same. Because it is collective, an archetype speaks across time and space. The classic tales handed down through the generations speak of values, of feelings felt, of risks taken, of life and death and what the character Zorba the Greek called "the whole catastrophe" of being human. Jack (of Beanstalk fame) and Luke Skywalker are brothers.

I found it at the movies

The twentieth century will certainly be remembered for its technological revolution. Yet it could just as easily be named the century of the story. Surely there has never been more storytelling per capita going on in history than there has been lately. Giant industries are spewing forth tales at an overwhelming rate in books, magazines, newspapers, plays, movies, television shows, videos, CDs and DVDs, interactive multimedia programs, and computer software. These are only a few ways that stories march through our lives. Add to that the narrative environment of the theme park, the sermons and homilies delivered in churches, temples, and mosques every week, and the homespun family history passed down from generation to generation.

Storytelling is about drama, and drama is about emotions. Like you, I learned early on that emotions that were unacceptable in life were okay at the movies. I could cry, feel angry, get terrified, giggle, and feel all sorts of things if I was watching someone else's life. Have you ever noticed how accessible your feelings become when you are seated in a darkened theater or in front of the television set? As an art therapist, I've been amazed at the therapeutic value of movies, especially for those who have trouble getting to their emotions. I once knew a successful businessman named Lyle who couldn't cry to save his soul but broke out in sobs while watching an old TV rerun movie about baseball star Lou Gehrig and his untimely death from the disease that bears his name. "I haven't cried like that since I was a kid," Lyle told me. "I'm shocked over the effect this film had on me. I didn't even cry like that when my wife left me. You're a therapist. What do you think is going on? Am I losing it?"

When I asked Lyle a little more about his feelings regarding Lou Gehrig's story, his own tale unfolded. He had been a star in high school baseball and had aspired to a career in sports. A professional team had even tried to recruit him. His career was suddenly cut short when both parents died in an accident, leaving him to support his younger brother. His career in business began, but his baseball ambitions died at the same time. He had never mourned the death of the baseball player he might have been. "No, Lyle, to answer your question, I don't think you're losing it. Rather I'd say you are finding it. Your real feelings."

Several months later Lyle called me excitedly. "I've started doing things I'd been postponing for years, like traveling, writing, and doing photography. I got a great camera and we just got back from Hawaii. You know," he continued, "I think I was afraid to feel and follow my heart because of the pain over losing that early dream. It was like, if you love to do something it will be taken away. So don't even go there." Then he laughed. "You're right. I did find something—my feelings, and I am expressing them more. I am a lot more relaxed, too, and my marriage has definitely improved. This trip was like a second honeymoon."

If you'd like to read more about the therapeutic value of stories in general, there is Michael Gurian's book *What Stories Does My Son Need?* A very informative book about stories told on celluloid is Gary Solomon's *The Motion Picture Prescription: Watch This Movie and Call Me in the Morning.* It includes guidance on the therapeutic value of films through short descriptions and thematic information. Let's face it: Movies are the dominant storytelling art of our time, so we might as well use them to inspire inner work through the expressive arts.

The next activity is designed for starting the process of finding more of yourself in the movies that move you.

FEELINGS IN THE MOVIES

Materials

Journal and felt pens

Activity

1. Using your *dominant hand,* write about a movie that deeply affected you.

   - What was the movie?
   - How did you feel about the movie?
   - What feelings came up as you watched it? Did you express those feelings at the time? How?
   - What was it about the movie that affected you? The plot? The characters? A particular scene?

2. If a character in the movie had a big impact on you, write an imaginary conversation with him or her. Your voice is written with your *dominant hand,* the character speaks through your *nondominant hand.* Imagine that you are face-to-face with this character.

   - What do you say?
   - What does the character say?

   Don't think about it, just let the pen move across the page. Allow this to be completely spontaneous.

3. With your *dominant hand,* jot down in your journal any observations you made about your reflections on this film and about your dialogue.

Writing from the still image

As you've already discovered, writing about nonverbal art and film images can help you name your feelings and gain greater insight into yourself. But there is far more you can do with words and pictures using still photographs as the jumping-off point for personal storytelling. You have a vast resource of photo images available to you in the form of popular magazines. Better yet, this source of images is inexpensive or even free (if you collect old magazines from friends or the doctor's office, barber shop, or beauty salon). By creating collages with magazine photos, graphic images, and words, it is possible to weave your own inner story much the way you do in the dream state. Sometimes such collages can be quite surreal, echoing the nonlinear, nonrational nature of dreams. In short, this is a right-brain frame of mind that invites you to dig deep into the unconscious for guidance, insight, and creative inspiration.

Out of my work with photo-and-word collage I have developed a form of storytelling that I call image writing. In this form, we allow ourselves to use photo-collage art as the cue for unfolding a tale from the Inner Self. It's like having a dream on paper.

AN IMAGE IS WORTH A THOUSAND WORDS

Materials

Collage materials (art paper, magazines, scissors, and glue), journal, and felt pens

Activity

1. Create a magazine-photo collage of an emotionally charged event or situation in your life (past or present). You can even do a collage of an emotion such as anger, joy, fear, sadness, peace, etc. Let the colors, images, and shapes express your experience of the theme you've selected.

2. Look at your completed collage. Allow any feelings that come up in response to it.

3. With your *nondominant hand,* let your picture speak in words in your journal. Allow the writing to be completely spontaneous. Don't try to correct it or determine what form it will take. This is free writing.

4. With your *dominant hand,* jot down in your journal any insights you had while doing the collage and image writing.

The night of the Los Angeles earthquake in 1994, Jeanette and Don were not far from the epicenter. Their house was devastated. At a workshop a few weeks later, Jeanette did a collage about her experience.

She then wrote a poem/story to illustrate her picture.

The Vision Beyond the Rubble

Croak, rumble, bang, crash
Rumble, rumble, rumble
Are you there? Are you there?
The walls, the fireplace, the family treasures
Reduced to rubble.
As far as you can see
Nothing but rubble.

Eventually the light of day and the
      sun beyond.

Where do you start? Must you start?

Brick and plaster, china and crystal
Back to the earth to start afresh.

The light glows beyond. There is light.

A new beginning, a fresh day.
The beauty of a new home

Lovely where the rubble once lay
Flowers and trees and light

There is always light beyond the destruction.

Later, when Jeanette showed her picture and read her written piece in the group sharing, she described the horror of being shaken awake to a totally pitch-black night. All the electricity was out, so they could only hear the sounds: the house creaking and cracking and objects smashing to the floor. They could tell that everything was being devastated. When they could finally see it, Don and Jeanette realized that "everything had been reduced to rubble."

In the aftermath of the quake, there were constant aftershocks to deal with as well as the business of getting on with their lives. Jeanette's collage and story express so poignantly the inner meaning of the experience—how it tested her will to live, her ability to create beauty where there had been destruction, to find a new life where there had been so much terror, pain, and grief.

Jeanette's sharing had a profound impact on everyone in the room, whether or not they had experienced the earthquake firsthand. Many said that the collage and poem/story expressed important passages in their own lives: divorces, near-death experiences, and other major crises. Jeanette's insight of finding "light beyond the destruction" spoke to the hearts of everyone in the group. It is a message of healing and hope: an eternal issue for humanity—death and rebirth, letting go of the past and beginning again.

At the end of Chapter Ten you will find another wonderful example of image writing based on a collage and dialogue. Done by a man named Christian, the story that unfolded from his collage images got him in touch with his inner wisdom, Inner Artist, and more. By finding images that portrayed these aspects of his personality and letting them speak, he did some powerful healing. He also created a new script for his future.

Writing from feelings

Another way to allow emotions to speak is to let them tell their own story. Many feelings have a long and complex history in our lives. Certain emotions that were not acceptable when we were growing up may have been embraced later in life. It's as if we have a relationship with each one of those emotions. We may have been at odds with certain feelings and more comfortable with others. The following journal activity can help you get in touch with how you react in the face of certain emotions. More important, it can pave the way for greater acceptance of all your emotions, no matter what they are.

FEELINGS TELL THEIR STORY

Materials
   Journal and felt pens

Activity
1. With your *nondominant hand,* write down the names of emotions that you have had difficulty with or have attempted to avoid or hide in some way.
2. With your *nondominant hand,* let each emotion speak. Let it tell its story about its role in your life—past, present, and future.
3. With your *dominant hand,* jot down any insights you have from these autobiographical writings.
4. With your *dominant hand,* write a story about the most joyful event in your life.

   - Where were you?
   - What happened externally?
   - What happened inside you?

5. Allow a happy emotion to speak to you, such as peace, tranquillity, serenity, joy, enthusiasm, etc. Let it write with your *nondominant hand.*

A woman writes about how she had squelched her natural enthusiasm and joie de vivre as she grew up. In order to be like the other kids her age, during adolescence she adopted a cool exterior. Her hidden enthusiasm had a lot to tell her.

Enthusiasm speaks.

I'm your enthusiasm. When you were little you could express me openly and easily, but when you got to be a teenager, you really shut down. You were supposed to be "cool" and it wasn't cool to show a lot of excitement. So I really got hidden away. You felt deeply about things, but it just wasn't cool to let it show.

Then in your late thirties you started having bouts of depression. Keeping me locked up all those years just caught up with you. I wanted to come out. I was dying to express myself and if you didn't let me, *you* were going to die. Fortunately for you *and* me, you started writing about your feelings and thoughts: what you wanted and what you didn't want. You came back to life and started taking singing lessons just for fun. That changed everything. And you got into a job you really like, finally. I'm out now and I'm not going back into hiding, ever.

Observation:

I see that it has been my enthusiasm that has served me in my new career in sales. It's infectious. People want to do business with me because I'm really excited about what I'm doing. Enthusiasm is just energy. I might as well use it. As they say, use it or lose it.

Writing as medicine

An April 26, 1999, *Newsweek* story by Claudia Calb entitled "Pen, Paper Power!" proclaims that "confessional writing has been around at least since the Renaissance, but new research suggests that it's far more therapeutic than anyone ever knew." The article goes on to describe ongoing medical research that began in the mid-1980s that linked writing about upsetting experiences and illnesses with strengthening of the immune system, fewer doctor visits, and improved health in general. Writing about such experiences has also been shown to increase levels of disease-fighting lymphocytes circulating in the bloodstream, and it may cause modest declines in blood pressure for those who need to lower theirs.

I had the opportunity to meet one of the pioneers in this research a number of years ago. James Pennebaker, psychology professor at the University of Texas in Austin, is one of the front-runners in the field of health and expressive writing. He has been a longtime supporter of my work and immediately saw the connection between drawing about trauma and writing about it. His work has been documented in his book *Opening Up: The Healing Power of Confiding in Others.*

More recent studies conducted at the State University of New York at Stony Brook have shown similar results. A group of 112 patients suffering with arthritis and asthma spent a total of one hour writing. For three days in a row in twenty-minute sessions, two-thirds of the group wrote about traumatic events such as auto accidents, being raped, being fired, or the death of a loved one. Some even cried while they wrote. The other participants were asked to write about their plans for the day. Four months later, nearly 50 percent of those who wrote about stressful events had improved significantly, as compared to 24.3 percent of those who wrote their daily plan. Dr. David Spiegel, a Stanford University psychiatrist, commenting on this research, observed that a minimal psychological social interaction can have very substantial medical effects. He believes that stress may play a role in the progression of illnesses like arthritis and asthma.

My own clinical experience with thousands of clients, students, and readers of my books on healing have confirmed that people almost invariably feel physically and emotionally better after writing about feelings, trauma, and painful situations. Sometimes the healing can occur in just one session, as in the case of Lucille and Pamela, whom you read about in Chapter Three. If you are interested in reading more case studies on how the Creative Journal method has helped heal chronic and acute conditions, see my books *The Picture of Health: Healing Your Life with Art* and *The Power of Your Other Hand.* My audiotape series, *The Wisdom of Your Other Hand,* also has case studies demonstrating how writing can release emotional tension and clear physical symptoms.

In addition to alleviating symptoms and improving our health, writing out our fears may also help with our performance at school and work. A study of students preparing for graduate school entrance exams was conducted at Carnegie-Mellon University by psychologist Stephen J. Lepore. All the students reported fears and anxiety about the test. Those who wrote about everything they'd done in the last twenty-four hours felt the same after the assignment. By contrast, students who were asked to write about their emotions felt significantly better afterward. I have seen the same results in creative journal programs I've conducted in public schools (K–12).

I truly believe that in expressing our hurts, fears, and pain we become stronger, both physically and emotionally. Life is our great teacher. It hands us challenges at every turn. How the story of our life turns out depends on how we respond to life situations. Writing about the most difficult times can pay great dividends, as my own clinical work and the medical studies show. So give it a try. You have nothing to lose but your pain and stress.

In expressing our deepest experiences through art and storytelling, we honor our humanity. Often this involves acknowledging our vulnerability and helplessness in the face of certain events and situations. Yet we can also find strength and beauty in "a new beginning, a fresh day."

By honoring our human condition through the arts, we heal ourselves. We embrace our deepest fears and our greatest strength, what is most human and, at the same time, most divine in us.

LIFE AS TEACHER, EMOTIONS AS HEALERS

Materials

Journal and felt pens

Activity

1. With your *dominant hand,* write about a traumatic or painful event in your life. Include any feelings that come up as you write.

   • What happened?
   • How did you feel at the time?
   • How do you feel about it now?

   Note: If you are a survivor of child abuse or other violent crime, do this activity with a professional or with a trusted friend present.

2. Ask your Inner Wisdom Guide to help you with the feelings and memories that came up. Ask it for any comfort or wisdom that you need right now. Your voice is written with your *dominant hand,* and the voice of your Inner Wisdom Guide is written with your *nondominant hand.* You may want to create a drawing or collage of this Inner Guide before writing.

3. If you feel comfortable sharing your picture and writing with someone who is safe for you, a person who does not judge or criticize you, go ahead. Sometimes people share this work with a therapist, spouse, or best friend. Just be sure the person is accepting of you and your feelings.

Journal example:

I was almost killed in a car accident many years ago while crossing a busy city street. I can still remember what I had on. A sunflower yellow summer dress and butterscotch-colored shoes. Funny how details like that will stick in your mind years later. The odd thing is that I don't remember the actual impact. I must have left my body or something because I never saw the car coming. Seconds later I was sitting in the middle of the street with blood on my dress, thinking, How clumsy, I must have tripped. It was a long time before I could walk across a street without being scared to death inside. I feel very vulnerable remembering this and realizing how close death was that day.

Inner Guide:

I was there with you that day. I took you out of your body so that you wouldn't remember the car hitting your leg and throwing you up in the air. You didn't need that memory on top of the physical pain you had for weeks afterward and the abrasions on your face. You were protected and you still are. You are a child of God, and, although life gives you lessons, you are here to learn and be strengthened by them. Your task is to truly understand that—to love yourself and others.

Listening to the guide within

Expressing your real self—your true feelings, personal experiences, and insights—can become a spiritual practice. In fact, writing as a spiritual practice is not new. The twelve-step program's fourth step is a written personal inventory, which helps develop honesty and a sense of self-observation. The soul and spirituality are old friends to the writing process. The diaries of great beings, not to mention holy scripture from every spiritual tradition, contain words that have healed, inspired, and lifted the spirit for centuries. The ecstatic poet saints of the East, like Rumi, Kabir, Hafiz, sages such as Lao Tzu, along with Western mystics like St. Teresa of Avila, St. John of the Cross, and Hildegard of Bingen bear witness to the transcendent quality of writing from the source. Getting out of the way, we can allow the deepest well of understanding and love to pour out through our hands in the form of words.

MAKING THE INVISIBLE VISIBLE

Materials

Journal and felt pens

Activity

1. With your *dominant hand,* ask your Inner Wisdom Guide to counsel you about anything in your life that is troubling you at this time. Ask the questions with your *dominant hand,* and let your Inner Wisdom Guide respond with your *nondominant hand.*

2. Write a letter or prayer of thanksgiving to the source of wisdom and creativity that lives within you. Thank it for all your emotions and ask it to bless you and them. Use whichever hand you wish.

3. With your *dominant hand,* journal any reflections and insights about expressive writing and its benefits in your life.

Storytelling through the expressive arts is a beautiful way to bring the unconscious realm of images, movement, color, and sound out into the conscious world of words. Through words we find the voice of our Inner Wisdom Guide and speak our truth. It is a way to really listen to the "still small voice within."

9. FACING OURSELVES: MASK MAKING AND INNER DIALOGUES

Finding our many selves

According to many schools of psychology, we each carry within us different subpersonalities. Each aspect of our personality has its own values, likes and dislikes, and set of feelings. Each subpersonality is reflected in our behavior or in the many roles we play. Clarette has a well-developed Achiever self, a Mother self, an Organizer, and a Spiritual Seeker, but her Playgirl, Artist, and Couch Potato roles are completely missing. Consequently, she is overly responsible and suffers from chronic fatigue. She needs some rest and recreation. Yet the parts of her—the Playgirl, Artist, and Couch Potato—that would enable her to take time off for self-nurturing are all in the closet. She has disowned them and feels uncomfortable when they try to speak. She usually has to get sick in order to take time off from work and other community obligations. Being sick in bed, she can give herself permission to read novels (which she usually dismisses as frivolous) and to write poetry, a talent she has ignored in her adult years. Clarette's inner conflict about being overworked expresses itself as fatigue and illness. Sickness is a high price to pay for a rest and for balancing parts of ourselves.

With people like Clarette, I suggest subpersonality work to get at the bottom of the obvious imbalance in their lives. We inevitably find that a few subpersonalities have been ignored and have not been allowed to be expressed in the individual's life. They are simply crying out for attention.

There are unlimited numbers of these subpersonalities inside each of us. Whether we study Jungian psychology, Assagioli's Psychosynthesis, or Hal and Sidra Stone's Voice Dialogue method, we see the same picture of the psyche. A cast of characters makes up our inner theater.

Jung believed that we each have within us all of the archetypes, for they are in our collective unconscious as a human race. This is what makes it possible for us to have understanding and compassion for one another. We are all made of the same archetypal stuff. However, when we disown any of these inner characters, trouble results. We engage in what psychologists call projection. The feelings and traits we have judged as unacceptable in ourselves get projected onto others and we point accusing fingers. The Workaholic within us is the first to judge someone else who values and enjoys leisure time. Sometimes we see our unacknowledged talents in others and fall into idol worship. The Procrastinator may admire someone who identifies with an Achiever self. In either case, we take the spotlight off ourselves and put the personality trait "out there." We think the other person has it and we don't.

Subpersonalities and emotions

The reason that subpersonalities are so important when working with emotions is that each aspect of our personality has its own feelings and worldview. They are quite different from each other, and their values may be in stark contrast. This can lead to inner conflict. We describe it as *being of two minds,* or we *can't make up our mind,* or we *feel torn.* For example, the Achiever self wants to accomplish more and faster. Picture the modern cell-phone–chatting, laptop-toting jet-setter ambitiously keeping to a hectic schedule. On the other hand, the Beach Bum self may want to go on an extended vacation and do nothing but hang out on the beach. If the Achiever self takes over a person's life, burnout or some other stress disorder may result, as in Clarette's case.

A conscious life involves awareness of all of these parts of the self. The real drama is the one within: the conflicts and resolutions we experience with all the characters and mixed emotions that live within us. When Shakespeare said "All the world's a stage," he might as well have been talking about the individual human psyche as well as the outer world.

So let's go on a treasure hunt to find some parts of yourself that carry strong emotions. Through imagery and written dialogues, you will get to know who these subpersonalities are, how they feel, and what they need from you. You have already used many of these techniques in the context of body dialogues and art making. Now you will expand the work into creating characters and giving them a voice. We will start with a collage and image-writing activity and then move on to mask making and more dialogues.

MAKING FACES, PART I

Materials

Art paper, drawing or painting supplies, or photo-collage materials, journal, and felt pens

Activity

1. Sit quietly and focus on an emotion you would like to explore. It can be one you are struggling with, or it may be one you would like to cultivate, such as playfulness or joy. Or perhaps it is an emotion you avoid expressing and would like to be more comfortable with, such as anger or sadness.

2. With your *nondominant hand,* draw a picture of a character who personifies this emotion. You can do the drawing in your journal or on a large sheet of art paper if you wish. It's up to you. Or you can create the character through collage by using magazine photos (see example below).

3. Write an interview with the character. Ask the questions with your *dominant hand.*
    Respond with your *nondominant hand,* using contrasting colors for the character.
    Some questions to ask are:

    - What is your name?
    - Can you tell me about yourself?
    - How do you feel?
    - What do you do for me?
    - Is there anything you want from me?

Example

Who are you? There are two of you? Can you tell me about yourselves?

Girl dancing:

> *I'm Playanna. I look like I'm in a woman's body, but I'm really about five or so.
> I love to dance and go to parties and skip and roller-skate and have fun. But you
> don't do it very much. So I'm trying to
> come out and remind you about the
> things you really love to do.*

Little girl with a teddy bear:

> *I'm Little Dreamer, the kid sister of that
> one that's dancing over there. I like to
> take naps and cuddle with my teddy
> and sleep in a big pretty bed.*

What do you girls do for me?

Girl dancing:

> *I bring play and fun into your life. I
> know how to have a good time. Without
> me things can get pretty grown-up and
> dull and boring.*

Little girl with a teddy bear:

> *I'm the one who gives you peace and quiet and cozy feelings in your heart. I know how to dream, too.*

Have you girls told me what you want?

Girl dancing:

> *Yes, I've been telling you. You did take me roller-skating this summer, but then you forgot about it. I have to keep telling you. But you are taking a dance class and I'm happy about that. And you let me wear pretty clothes. I love to play dress-up. But I want more roller-skating and I want you to find a friend to skate with.*

Little girl with teddy bear:

> *You let me take naps and cuddle up in bed sometimes, but usually you have to get real tired before you do that. Or sometimes you get sick before I can really come out. I want you to just cuddle up in bed with me and sleep late sometimes and even spend a morning in bed (on the weekend).*

Mask making and our many selves

One of my favorite media for exploring subpersonalities through the arts is mask making. The roles we play and the subpersonalities we identify with can be dramatically revealed through faces that we create. This is a wonderful way to find the parts of ourselves that we have yet to discover. A case in point is Jane, a woman in her early sixties. Actually, Jane's story highlights the value of working with both clay and mask making for creating life transformations.

Until her early forties, Jane had been a full-time homemaker, wife, and mother. After recuperating from surgery necessitated by a life-threatening medical condition, Jane began exploring clay for the first time, using the potter's wheel and kiln that her ceramist mother had given her. She said she "loved the feel of clay right from the start." She also began taking yoga classes and says it was the combination of clay and yoga that helped her heal and also see that her marriage was dead and could not be saved. She divorced and began the next chapter in her life.

Jane worked as a legal secretary and assistant for many years, but all of her free time was devoted to working with clay. She became a skilled potter, showing and selling her work. She had thought of turning to ceramics professionally but realized that it would involve manufacturing and that the product would become more important than the creative process. As she puts it, "I decided not to quit my day job." Yet the job was not fulfilling. A few years went by and Jane attended a yoga retreat in which Tarot-like pictures in the Spirit Card deck were used for divination. She drew the Painted Face card, signifying finding your own Medicine (power) and allowing it to emerge. A year later, at another workshop, she made a mask. Without intending to, she created her own version of the Painted Face she'd drawn from the Spirit Card deck a year earlier. More would be revealed.

She wrote the following poem about her mask:

The Painted Face
speaks of allowing
the Medicine of
Self to emerge

Nostrils are open,
breath is life,
Eyes are closed,
passionate inner vision
brings transformation.

The Painted Face
speaks of opening,
productive change,
love and healing.

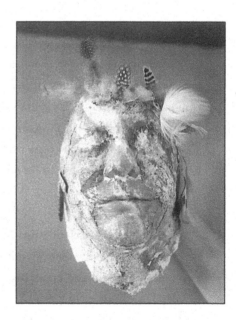

A year later she attended a weekend workshop on the Hawaiian Huna tradition, "The Way of the Adventurer Shaman." She was introduced to body-centered psychotherapy and spent the next two years as a client, clearing old patterns. Around that time she also made three little-girl figures in clay. They turned out to be her Inner Child expressing fear, sadness, and loneliness. These feeling states emerged out of the clay by complete surprise. She had found the roots of incapacitating fears and constriction that had been lodged in her body-mind. Seeing these old fears reveal themselves in the clay allowed Jane to feel them and let the restrictions and immobility go. Empowered to move forward with her life, she trained and eventually became a practitioner of body-mind work. She had found her Medicine (power). And when she began doing bodywork in the training, her first impression was: "This is like working with clay."

MAKING FACES, PART 2

Materials

Plaster cloth strips (such as Activa brand, available at arts, crafts, or hobby stores), Vaseline for coating the face, bowl of warm water, towel to lie down on, towel for cleaning up. (You may want to put a plastic drop cloth under the whole area as well, as you don't want any of the plaster that's in the gauze to get onto the floor or carpet.) Note: You will need another person to shape the mask to the contours of your face. If you don't have anyone to help you, there are suggestions for other mask-making alternatives below.

Activity

1. Cut the plaster cloth strips into pieces a few inches long. Apply the Vaseline to your entire face and neck with your fingers. Lie down on the floor with a towel under your head and upper part of your body. Set the bowl of water next to where you are.

2. Your helper will apply the plaster cloth strips to your face. He or she dips the cloth strips into the water, wringing them out enough to remove the excess water. He or she lays them in several layers on your face, leaving a space around your eyes for an opening to see through. After the mask has been formed on your face, lie still for about a half hour as the mask hardens.

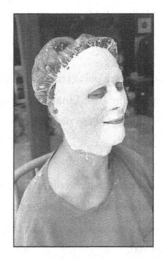

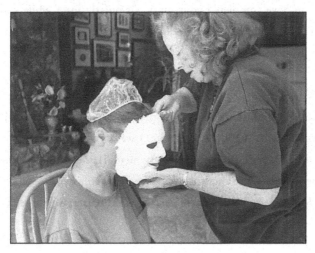

3. When the mask has hardened, gently lift it off your face and set it aside to dry even more. It is best to wait a while before attempting any further work on the mask surface, like painting, collage, etc. You want the mask to be very firm and dry before continuing. It's best to wait a few hours or dry it overnight.

MAKING FACES, PART 3

Materials

Small jars of tempera paint (six to eight colors) or set of tube watercolors, brush, jar of water, white liquid glue (like Elmer's), collage materials (tissue paper, ribbons, yarn, cellophane, odds and ends of scrap paper, fabric, feathers, magazine photos, etc.)

Activity

1. Complete your plaster mask by painting and decorating it. You can also collage colors and shapes onto it and create hair or other elements around the face with three-dimensional materials such as yarn, cellophane, fabric, feathers, paper, etc. (see illustrations).

2. When you have completed your mask, sit quietly for a while and contemplate it. Look at yourself in the mirror, wearing the mask.

3. In your journal:

   • Write a poem or piece about the mask with your *dominant hand.*
   • Let the mask speak in the first person present by writing with your *nondominant hand.* "I am. . . . I feel. . . . I want. . . ."
   • Did any emotions come up? Any memories? Any associations with other experiences? Write about it with your *dominant hand.*
   • How do you feel about this mask? What part(s) of your self does it portray?

4. Display your mask in an appropriate place. In your everyday life, honor the part(s) of you that this mask represents in any way that feels right.

5. Ask someone to take a picture of you wearing the mask.

Reflections on the Mask

Elation
Joyous
    rebirth
Harvesting
    the fruits
    of all the
    other births
    and
    rebirths
Spiraling
upward
opening
blossoming
one petal
one flower
at a time

The woman of darkness and light

This mask says: "I have both parts: a bright, cheery, extroverted nature—the teacher, the professional woman—but also a private, introverted one that feels deeply. The artist self resides here. She works in the dark, in mysterious ways that I can never fully comprehend. But I would be lost without her. She also has the healing power. She is a shaman.

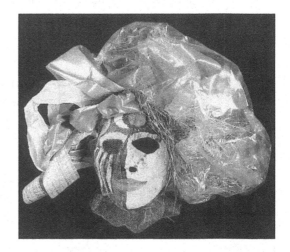

OTHER APPLICATIONS

Activity

By using the same method for making your mask form, you can do the following:

- Make an inner and outer self mask. Decorate both sides of the mask: The outside is the face you show to the world; the inside represents your private feelings.
- Express a conflict in your life through your mask: a divided face, or inside and outside.
- Make a feelings mask of an emotion with which you have trouble. Honor it by creating a little altar or sacred space for it, and ask your Creative Self to help you heal your relationship with this emotion.
- Create a mask of a part of yourself that you would like to develop, as with Jane's Painted Face that predated her discovery of the body-mind healer within.

Methods of mask making

As mentioned above, if making plaster-cast masks is not practical because you don't have a helper on hand, you can use some of the following materials for creating very simple masks. They won't all be contoured to fit your face, but they can reveal a great deal through painting and the other decorative elements you choose.

Other mask materials:

- paper plates
- large paper shopping bags placed over your head
- cardboard, poster board, or railroad board cut to fit the size of your face
- construction paper or heavy art paper
- ready-made white masks available in craft stores

The Black Wizard Mask was made by Susan with fabric stretched over a cardboard backing.

A wonderful example of a paper bag mask appears in the next chapter as part of a case study of Christian, a young man who was dealing with fear and anger. (See story in Chapter Ten.)

The following are Susan's written reflections on the mask-making process:

Although I was very excited about doing the masks, I was aware of resistance on my part. I did not focus on the exercise until the night before and I got the directions all wrong. I spent two hours in the evening before the workshop day actively gathering ideas and materials. Then I went to bed. I felt clear that I knew where I was going.

I had a dream relating to the mask workshop. Spiders have always been metaphors for my fears, and webs and spiders appear a lot. For the last few years, the spiders have become smaller and the webs old and no longer used. Sometimes the spiders are funny, need comfort, or are harmless.

Dream: I'm in an old house, where each room is full of old unused spiderwebs; only a few very tiny spiders linger. There was an old heavy woman who was fearful of going outside. Her mean old husband wanted her to stay inside. I pulled a knife on him and he also brandished a knife at me. At this point, *she* got strong with me, grabbed me, and I felt how very strong *she is*.

At the workshop I made this mask. The name, Black Wizard, came first. This was my response to the mask, written with my dominant hand.

This mask represents a strong, dangerous, sexual woman—the beauty of the female in her powers, the lioness protecting the young, the magic and wizardry of the Medicine Woman.

She represents all that is hidden from view, the spiritual and the physical come together in her. She holds within her deep emotion, and the physical response is sexual.

Stealth	Claiming your own
Power	Owning your power
Life	
Beauty	
Mystery	
Darkness	
Danger	
Daring	
Balance	

Left hand:
I am strong. I am power-full. I am brave.
    I can outsmart you.
I am clever
I am not nice.
    I have wisdom
I get what I want
earth
    dark
    void
    death

This mask represents the culmination of a long journey to reveal myself completely. To claim and own fully my being, my weakness and my power. To step up and take my place, to walk my talk, to be the conscious, real, magic person I am.

I have powerful Medicine (power) which asks that you also claim the power, and I have run from this many times. This entire year has been full of events that have taken me closer to fully revealing this part of self and honoring her.

I love my mask.

Joy, enthusiasm, and playfulness

Once you have begun exploring the world of three-dimensional expressive arts, you may be pleasantly surprised at what you discover, not only in yourself but also in the art materials. These are the kinds of activities your Inner Child loves.

    Some years ago when I was dealing with illness, some friends brought back a very special gift from Bali. It was a mask of a smiling face. I had been feeling very depressed,

Try the "making faces" activity or any other mask-making method for fully expressing feelings of joy, happiness, playfulness.

and my energy was at an all-time low. Just looking at the mask made me feel better. I decided to place it on the mantel of my fireplace where I could see it all day. There it sat, next to my Quan Yin statue (representing feminine compassion and the nurturing mother), beaming down joy and good humor. It reminded me of the light side of life, something it had been hard to do when facing such a debilitating illness. I think of it as "mask therapy," and it certainly helped lift my spirits. I believe that the Balinese mask maker who created this magical face had transferred some very strong shamanic medicine into this exquisite work of art.

Collecting masks from different cultures can be a wonderful way to receive inspiration for creating your own. My collection includes:

- a beaded sun/moon from the Huichol Indians
- a mask depicting an Australian Aboriginal shaman that appeared in a friend's dream about my illness and healing
- two birthday masks made especially for me by artist, friend, and co-author Peggy Van Pelt
- an Italian ceramic sun/moon mask
- a Venetian painted leather mask used for Carnevale
- a black Buddha mask made of wood
- a papier-mâché mask of the Hindu elephant/child god Ganesh

These might give you some ideas about masks you'd like to collect. Contemplating the personal meaning of masks, what they represent and the emotions they convey, can be almost as revealing as creating your own. Many mask artists seem to hit a deep vein of universal emotions that cut across cultures, distance, and even time. A visit to the largest mask museum in the world, in Zacatecas, Mexico, illuminated for me the common threads that hold us all together. The Cleveland Museum of Art also has a wonderful collection of masks from various indigenous cultures. Of course, the city of masks is Venice, Italy. There are whole shops there dedicated to this ancient art form. In viewing these collections one realizes that underneath the masks of race, color, creed, or nationality, we still share the same humanity.

Exploring the selves through Voice Dialogue

One method I find valuable for exploring subpersonalities is the Voice Dialogue method, developed by Drs. Hal and Sidra Stone. In their approach, the therapist or facilitator actually interviews the subpersonalities of the other individual. Referred to as voices, these subpersonalities take their place in different areas of the room. They each speak in the first person, one at a time. This method always starts with addressing an aware ego (or decision maker of the psyche), followed by the selves that constellate around it. The goal is to develop the awareness of the aware ego and put it in its rightful place as the decision maker. Like a chairman of the board, the aware ego must make choices, such as what job to accept, what house to rent, whom to marry, and so forth. Ignoring or denying any one of the selves (or voices) is courting emotional disaster. It would be like a chairman of the board ignoring the opinions and concerns of the other board members.

The selves who are not invited to the inner round table of the psyche will be outside in the unconscious making trouble. The dark fairy who cast the spell over Sleeping Beauty was the one who was not invited to the princess's christening. In her anger at being left out, she put a hex on the whole kingdom. In real life when parts of us are ignored, they get our attention through such things as unexpected emotional outbursts, debilitating depression, or stress-related illnesses that interfere with the flow of our lives. We ignore the different parts of ourselves at our own peril.

As a trained Voice Dialogue facilitator, I have used this picture of the psyche as the theoretical framework for my own work in expressive arts. Over and over again, I have seen dramatic transformations as individuals have spontaneously moved around the room to find the many parts of themselves. Voice Dialogue brings awareness of our primary selves (subpersonalities running the show) as well as silent (disowned) parts. By honoring them all, we learn what they have to give us. This kind of awareness is the royal road to becoming more fully human. It is also the cure for ailing relationships. Acknowledging our primary selves while also learning to embrace the closeted parts definitely improves how we relate to others. Voice Dialogue work with subpersonalities is great in families and work teams. It helps us remove our projections onto others. I strongly recommend the following books by Hal and Sidra Stone. They should be read only in the order given: *Embracing Our Selves* and *Partnering*.

The Stones have also created many excellent recordings that include theory and application, and they conduct workshops and intensives. (See the Resources for more information.)

You do need a partner in order to do Voice Dialogue work, and this requires some training. But you don't have to be a therapist to do it, and individuals can learn to facilitate each other. As for doing the work on your own, there is much to be gained from simply reading about the method and observing your own subpersonalities in action. In addition, there is my own application of Voice Dialogue principles through the journal dialogues you've been doing in this book. The technique of drawing portraits of subpersonalities and writing dialogues using both hands is Voice Dialogue on paper. The nondominant hand always speaks for voices that have been disowned: These are often the Inner Child, Inner Artist, the body, the Inner Wisdom Guide. The dominant hand speaks for the heavyweights that are more domineering: the Inner Critic, Perfectionist, Pusher, etc. The dominant hand also speaks for the primary selves (those aspects of our personality that we identify with) and for the aware ego.

In the Creative Journal method, the reflective writing that follows both portrait drawing and dialoguing takes us to the part of us that, in Voice Dialogue, is termed witness state. That's the part that silently observes without judgment and can see the big picture. Drawing on this state of witnessing, we can then do journal writing about current issues. In doing so, we look at the big picture and cultivate our aware ego, who can make more informed choices in daily life situations. Writing our reflections on these dialogues using the dominant hand enables the aware ego self to observe, decide, and bring about action. The aware ego always writes with the dominant hand.

Written dialogues have proven highly valuable for getting to the bottom of internal conflicts, especially when we have mixed emotions. We ask the question: Which sub-personality is behind this particular emotion? Then we get to know that part of our-self, embrace it, and allow its healthy expression in our lives. In this way we achieve inner balance and a broader range of life experience.

10. ACCEPTING YOUR FEELINGS: LETTING GO OF JUDGMENT

Remember the story about the man who mistook the rope for a snake? His distorted perception caused him to react, both emotionally and physically, as if there were a clear and present danger. When he saw the truth, he had a change of mind. And his feelings and body followed suit. The same is true regarding our beliefs about ourselves. How we see ourselves determines how we feel and how we experience life. We can change our lives by changing our minds.

Negative beliefs about ourselves have an impact on our emotions and our bodies. Limiting attitudes make us tired and old before our time and severely restrict our relationships and our lives. They shrink us down and put us in a box. In this chapter, we'll be looking at the subpersonalities that carry negative attitudes and beliefs about ourselves. By negative, I mean the ones that make us feel inadequate and less than who we really are or want to become. Such beliefs interfere with our current values, goals, and true heart's desires. In this chapter, you'll use all the expressive arts media you've experienced so far. You'll examine beliefs that no longer serve you and learn how to let go of them. More than that, you'll start the process of creating a life full of feeling and of dreams come true.

Clearing the emotions by clearing the mind

The mind contains beliefs and attitudes that affect our biochemistry and our emotions. What we believe about ourselves gives shape to our choices and behavior. Positive beliefs uplift the spirit, inspiring and energizing us. Henry Ford said, "If you think you can, you can." Walt Disney used to say, "If you can dream it, you can do it." We've all used the phrase, "Where there's a will there's a way." Or we talk about mind over matter. The power of the mind has been demonstrated by scientific medical research in what is called the placebo effect. In many studies, plain water or sugar pills are administered to patients who believe they are taking legitimate medication. Sizable percentages of patients in such groups actually improve or are cured of physical ailments. This illustrates the power of belief.

Medical studies have also demonstrated that a positive attitude can heal our emotions and our body. In his groundbreaking research many years ago, Dr. Carl O. Simonton found that the greatest predictor of a patient's healing was a positive outlook. Since then there has been ample research showing that a patient who has an attitude of self-efficacy or a belief in help from a higher healing power has a better chance of surviving a life-threatening or debilitating disease than a patient who does not.

Many years ago I witnessed a most dramatic case of how beliefs about the self affect behavior. A middle-aged man who was an abuse survivor had suffered with a severe stuttering problem all his life. A highly gifted and skilled artist, he had read about

Voice Dialogue and wanted a firsthand experience. In a workshop, his Inner Artist subpersonality began talking. He was not aware of it, but his stutter disappeared as if by magic. At the end of the session it was pointed out that his Inner Artist subpersonality was completely articulate and did not hesitate over so much as a syllable. In thinking back, he realized that this was true, and he was utterly amazed.

In discussing this phenomenon later, it made perfect sense. This man was a talented artist who loved to paint and draw and felt confident about his work. When he was engaged in art making, the pressure of trying to use words was removed because these activities do not require speech. He could relax and communicate through the language of line, shape, color, and texture. It was no wonder that his Inner Artist was articulate. This particular subpersonality was already expressing beautifully through nonverbal means and had been doing so for some years. It felt good about itself, but his talking self who had to speak to others did not.

Over and over again, in doing Voice Dialogue work with clients, I have observed different energies in people and how a subpersonality's beliefs and worldview can influence the emotions and the body. For example, the more critical, perfectionistic, and work-driven subpersonalities actually look older when the person is speaking from that voice. By contrast, the Inner Child has an unmistakable youthfulness about it. People who start accessing the Inner Child on a regular basis begin to look younger and more relaxed in their everyday lives.

In two of my previous books, *The Power of Your Other Hand* and *Recovery of Your Inner Child,* I included a photo of me joyfully riding a skateboard. I was thirty-nine years old when that picture was taken, and had just learned to skateboard. Everyone who sees it says the same thing: "You look about fifteen years old in that photo." My reply is always the same: "Of course, that's my Inner Child you're looking at." But I had to completely alter my beliefs about myself in order to get on that skateboard, much less be out riding it in public at my age.

In order to allow my Inner Child to come out and have the kind of fun she likes, I had to face my Critical Parent self and deal with its beliefs about myself and my role in life. I also had to overcome the prescribed attitudes I'd picked up from my family and society. These restrictive beliefs resided in the Inner Critic, who told me how unfitting it was for a woman of my age and station in life to be out skateboarding. "What if your college students see you?" it queried. "What if the college administrators spot you acting like a kid? What if your therapy clients catch you skateboarding? What will they think? After all, skateboarding is for teenage boys, not college graduates who are therapists, teachers, and parents of teenagers."

Another more survival-oriented parent voice in my head predicted that I would fall down and injure myself. It was no surprise that when I told my mother I had started skateboarding, her first reaction was, "My God, you'll fall down and break something." That overly cautious voice in my own head had been originally schooled by my mother, who had been quite overprotective about the physical safety of her only child. Her intentions were good (as were those of the overprotective voice in my head), but they limited the full expression of my playful, adventurous, and risk-taking sub-personalities.

Confronting my own Inner Parent voices in the journal enabled me to go out and play. The whole process was hard work but well worth the effort. The result was that my risk-taking and creative sides flourished in other areas of my life. I finished my first book during the time I began skateboarding. I also started taking dance classes for the first time. And I worked up the courage to send out my manuscript to publishers, eventually leading to publication. As simple a thing as allowing myself to skateboard prompted major leaps forward in my life as a fun-loving person and as an innovative professional. In working through my fears of looking foolish in the eyes of others and my terror of falling and hurting myself, I developed an inner strength that has served me in many areas of my life.

A change of mind

In exercising the power of the mind in a conscious way, we take charge of our lives. We choose where we want to go instead of leaving it up to some subpersonality who has taken control. In order to harness the power of the mind, there are some principles you need to be aware of.

- Your beliefs and attitudes affect your feelings and your body.
- You have the ability to examine your beliefs (be they conscious or unconscious) and the subpersonalities where they reside.
- You have the power to change your negative, self-defeating beliefs and attitudes by replacing them with positive, self-affirming ones.
- You can create new beliefs that support your true wishes by cultivating the subpersonalities that support your dreams.

In order to adopt more constructive beliefs, you first have to know what you believe about yourself. Many of your beliefs are so unconscious and ingrained that you may not even know what they are. Your first set of beliefs and attitudes was learned long ago in childhood from your parents, teachers, and other authority figures. For example, I was taught to avoid all physical risks out of fear that I would get hurt. At the same time, I grew up being told I was awkward and clumsy. So my Critical Parent within recorded this information and framed a belief: You should never take physical risks because you are awkward and will surely fall and get hurt. The result was chronic fear of any sports or activities involving possible injury. While realistic caution is good, obsessive fear about injury can severely limit our enjoyment of life. More limiting still is a negative self-image that says we are incapable of doing certain things. That's what had happened to me until I started reparenting myself, changing my beliefs and my behavior. Then I followed my Inner Child's desires and learned to dance, skateboard, and engage in other activities befitting a new self-image, that of a physically strong and graceful person.

The worldview of the adults in charge was given to you as a ready-made road map or life script. Expectations of who you are, how you should think, what you should believe, and how you should behave were handed to you at home, school, church or temple, and in the media. In growing up you also drew some of your own conclusions about the way the world works based on your life experience and perceptions.

Inner conflict arises when the old life script you've been operating from does not match your God-given talents and deepest longings at this particular time. How many true heart's desires have you had that never materialized? How many strongly felt wishes have you had that never came true? There was probably an old, outmoded belief about yourself that got in the way.

Some of your negative beliefs are unconscious, some of them are conscious. Either way, they can be changed. You do have a choice. It is possible to map out a unique and authentic life based on who you are now and who you want to become. This involves a relearning process: a change of mind and a change of heart. It also means really listening to your feelings. By honoring your true feelings, you can create new attitudes and beliefs about yourself, and new dreams.

A change of heart: nurturing yourself

Before learning to monitor negative self-talk and changing negative beliefs, you need to find a voice in your head that says positive, constructive things to you. This part of you is there but needs to be accessed consciously. It can best be described as a Nurturing Parent within who loves you and accepts your emotional and physical child self unconditionally. This part of you is responsible for the positive beliefs you already hold about yourself. Perhaps you are proud of your talent for cooking, your organizational skills, or your ability to listen to others. These positive messages from your Nurturing self make you feel good about yourself. This nurturing part of you supports your true wishes and dreams, encouraging you to follow your heart.

WITH ALL MY LOVE

Materials

Journal and felt pens

Activity

1. In your journal, write a love letter to yourself in the second person. Use your *dominant hand.* Let this come from the most loving, nurturing place in your heart. In the letter, express appreciation for yourself. You might want to mention talents and qualities you have developed. How about the way you have handled difficult situations and come out the better for it? (Optional: You can read your love letter into a tape recorder and then play it back to yourself.)

2. Make a list of self-nurturing things you can do for yourself:

   - activities you enjoy
   - nurturing people or pets you like spending time with
   - favorite places where you feel comfortable or like to have fun

   Put these things into your calendar so that they don't get ignored or pushed aside for "more important" things.

Examples:

Dear Self,

I want you to know how much I love you. Your courage and enthusiasm really warm my heart. You've been through lots of tests in your life and you've come through every time. I know that sometimes you lose confidence in yourself, especially when the Inner Critic gets on your case. But I'm here to remind you about how lovable and worthwhile you are. Others know it and tell you that all the time. But I want you to feel it. To really feel it deep inside.

Nurturing myself:

Walking in nature
Watching the sunset
Dancing
Long, leisurely baths
Listening to music
Seeing good movies
Having dinner with friends
Traveling to beautiful places
Spending time with friends, with my cat
Spending time at the beach
Drives in the mountains nearby

As we believe, so we feel: dropping old baggage

Once we have started listening to and honoring our true feelings, we are ready to take on our limiting negative beliefs. But how do we identify those beliefs? Some of them are unconscious and we're not even aware of them. One way to find them is by looking at chronic blocks, frustrations, and emotional pain, especially those that are long-standing. Like the buried emotions hidden under physical pain, our toxic beliefs are usually at the root of chronic painful emotions. In other words, what we believe often determines how we feel. A particular emotion that keeps revisiting us is often a symptom of a belief that does not serve us. One woman's depression and feelings of hopelessness had been there as long as she could remember. They were like quicksand that kept pulling her under. She was so stuck in them that she didn't know what life could be without them. It was like living in a room without windows or doors. She had no idea what sunlight was like. That is, until she started dropping the old baggage of outworn and debilitating beliefs and negative self-talk. She did this by facing the subpersonalities that carried these toxic beliefs: a Critic, a Perfectionist, a Pusher who drove her mercilessly to work harder and faster but said she would never measure up. She shifted her thinking through written dialogues with her subpersonalities using both hands.

Many schools of thought teach that we simply need to find our old, toxic beliefs and replace them with healthy ones. For example, a belief such as "I will never succeed in business for myself" is refashioned into a statement like "I have all the talent and support I need to succeed in my own business." Although this is a valuable exercise and I have incorporated such techniques into my earlier books, I have found that this isn't enough in itself. We still have to address the residual emotions that were caused by the negative self-talk. Superimposing positive affirmations on long-standing emotional reactions to our toxic beliefs is like icing a burnt cake. The new positive affirmations sound good, but what about the accumulated feelings that remain underneath?

There's another problem, too. If we don't uncover the subpersonality that carries the negative self-talk, it will create new negative beliefs. Maybe we rewrite the message that says we can't succeed in business, only to find that it's been replaced with another one that says: "You aren't spiritual enough" or "You'll never learn to meditate correctly." When that happens, you can be sure that a New Age Critic or a Personal Growth Pusher is lurking in the wings. New Age or Old Age, what's the difference? It's still the same critical voice that tells you how inadequate you are and that you'll never be enough.

Identifying and setting limits on the Critical Inner Parent in our own heads is like pulling weeds out by their roots. By contrast, without identifying the Critical Parent voice in our heads, verbal affirmations are like cutting weeds back at the ground. They will simply grow back, perhaps in another form with different words, but they will return.

The Critical Parent's negative self-talk is part of our Inner Family dynamics. If we can identify that part of us that creates and perpetuates negative beliefs about ourselves, it's easier to change those beliefs. A change of mind happens partly as a result of recognizing that nagging voice in our heads and setting limits on it. It also happens as a result of strengthening the Nurturing and Protective Parent within, who specializes in positive self-talk. This parent helps us with a change of heart and protects us from attack by the Critical Parent within.

Never forget that behind all our current negative self-talk is a Critical Parent in our own heads. It is the one who is doing the talking and telling us that we are no good and never will be. It is up to us to loosen its stranglehold. It has as much power as we give it, and we need to take our power back.

That isn't to say that all negative self-talk can be banished forever. This just isn't true. The Inner Critical Parent is always with us. It's part of the human condition. When I made this discovery, I started asking: What is the purpose of this Inner Critic? Does it do us any good? Why does it appear to be factory equipment for all humans? In an inner dialogue, I was told that the Critical Parent is like Kato in the *Pink Panther* movies. Kato was the martial arts expert that Inspector Clouseau hired to test his alertness at the most inopportune moments. Kato jumped out from behind doorways, from closets, through windows—springing at Clouseau with full force. Kato's appearance was always a surprise. It had to be; otherwise it would have been no test at all.

The Critical Parent voice in our heads started as a survival mechanism. It said, "Follow the rules. Be perfect; don't make mistakes. Play it safe." But when it indulges in character assassination—blaming and shaming our very essence—it crosses over the line and becomes the Critical Parent. Can we catch it in the act of damaging our self-esteem and self-confidence? Can we set limits on it? Can we put it in its place? That is what is being asked of us. When we wimp out in the face of the Critical Parent's diatribes, we give away our power and hide our strength and enthusiasm from ourselves and others. We end up with low energy, illness, depression, and emotions that linger on, such as chronic sadness, fear, anxiety, and anger. We may feel toxic guilt and shame, not for what we have done but for what we *are* at the very core of our being.

Our task is to identify the negative self-talk that emanates from our Inner Critical Parent subpersonality, to disidentify from it and to take things into our own hands. We do this by writing down what it says in the second person. "You are stupid" instead of "I am stupid." As long as we say "I am stupid" to ourselves, we identify with the critical attitude. Writing down "You are stupid" distances us from the Critic within, for that is how we heard put-downs from others. They said things like "You are stupid" and implanted that belief in our minds. When we use the second person, we see that the Critical Parent within is a separate voice, one that originally came from outside.

One way to begin disidentifying with the Inner Critic is to revisit the beginnings of negative self-talk in childhood. In the next activity you will return to childhood and shine the spotlight on negative messages about yourself that you heard from authority figures—parents, guardians, older adults, and siblings, etc. We are looking for the ones that were really character assassinations, where you were blamed and shamed and made to feel inadequate or totally worthless. Look for phrases like:

You lazy good-for-nothing.
You're a loser.
What a clumsy oaf.
You'll never amount to anything.
How could you be so stupid?
Where were you when they gave the brains out?
You're nothing but a spoiled brat.

Phrases like "You forgot to clean your room" don't qualify because they were just a statement about your behavior. On the other hand, "You're the messiest kid in the neighborhood. You're hopeless" is an attack on your character. These messages leave deep scars on our psyche. A valuable book on this subject is Byron Brown's *Soul Without Shame.*

Some critical messages you may have received were more subtle, such as comparisons made between you and a sibling or neighbor's child. You were made to feel "lesser than." And that is the true test of whether you were being judged. You *felt* put down. *Note: As with other activities in this book, if you encounter memories of severe abuse and feel overwhelmed with emotions while doing the next activity, stop. This could be a sign that you need help from a professional in dealing with these issues.*

HEALING THE PAST, PART I

Materials

Journal and felt pens

Activity

1. With your *dominant hand,* write a note to your Inner Child saying that you are go-ing to be going back to some times in childhood when you got hurt or experienced painful emotions. These may have been scary times, and going back to them in memory may bring up strong feelings. Reassure your Inner Child that he or she is not alone, that you will provide love and protection.

2. Go back in childhood and remember the put-down messages that were directed to you as a child. With your *dominant hand,* write them in your journal. Write them out as if you were transcribing a recording of someone talking to you:

    You are the sloppiest kid in the world.

    You must be the dumbest kid in school. Look at this report card.

    I can't believe how clumsy and awkward you are. You're hopeless.

3. Select one message from the list. With your *nondominant hand,* draw a picture of yourself as the child you were and of the person who said this to you. In other words, this is a portrait of someone putting you down. Draw a word cartoon bub-ble near the picture of the person who put you down. Inside the bubble, with your *dominant hand,* write the negative message.

4. Next to the picture of you as a child, write down emotion words that convey how you felt when you heard these messages. Write your feelings with your *nondominant hand.*

5. On a new page, allow the child in the picture to write more about how it feels be-ing talked to that way. Use your *nondominant hand* and write it in the present tense. Also feel free to write any other feelings or insights that come up.

Example

At the mercy of a dark and evil force.

Christian, a man in his early forties, drew this picture of a scene that repeated itself throughout his childhood. His child self is being assaulted by the father, who is completely beside himself with rage. To the boy it seems as if the father is possessed by some evil demons (shown as a dark head at the top right of the drawing). First came the father's abusive words shouted at the top of his lungs and then the physical beating.

Negative messages from the father before the beating took place:

You useless brat. Stop hiding. Where are you?
Come out at once. I'm going to beat good behavior into you.

How I felt:

Helpless. Hopeless. Nobody to rescue me. Horrified. Frozen to death with fear.
In looking at this drawing and expressing my Inner Child's feelings about the beatings from my father, I realized that I felt petrified at those times, and the horror stayed with me. Every time my father got agitated and talked loud, a feeling of horror would come over me. In fact, even today when anybody talks loudly in anger, I feel apprehension. All the alert signals go off. I still have the feeling when I'm around my father that if he weren't as old as he is, he could explode again just as he did in my childhood.

Healing the past, part 2

1. On a new page, let the Inner Child write down some of the messages it would have liked to hear in the situation pictured above. Use your *nondominant hand*. Then write any comments or observations with your *dominant hand*.

2. Repeat this process with as many of the put-down messages in part 1 as you wish. You may need more than one journal session to complete this.

Example

I realize that the beating usually followed something I did that was thoughtless or broke some rule. In these situations what I would have liked my father to say is:

Now, listen, son, we've got to talk together in privacy. Let's have a man-to-man talk.

I do love you, but you can't go around doing things like this. Let me explain. When you do _____, it affects other people. You can hurt others. When you're a kid, you don't always think about what you do and how it has an impact on others. But there are always consequences to your behavior.

I know that you have a good heart, but you can't go around doing these kinds of things without paying a price.

I really wanted reassurance from my father that I was lovable, no matter what. Observation (with dominant hand):

Now I see that I was a stand-in for my father's Inner Child. In beating me, he was really beating himself up. He was passing on to me what he got from his father. When my grandfather got mad, the whole house shook.

I realize that I am capable of breaking this vicious circle. I have the tools to establish a contact with my Inner Child and give it the love and protection it didn't get. I can now invite it out of the closet and let it speak for itself. I can respect it as an equal to my adult self with its own needs and wishes.

Clearing old patterns

Knowing where the negative self-talk in your head started is an important first step. However, in order to stop perpetuating this self-criticism, it is essential to see how those negative messages have been brought up to date by the Inner Critical Parent in your head today. For instance, an old message like "Your room is a mess; what a lazy slob you are" might now be worded as "Look at your desk at work; it's such a mess. You call yourself a professional? I always knew you were lazy and irresponsible."

Monitoring the self-destructive beliefs of the Inner Critical Parent is the key. Bringing them out into the open and putting them in their place reduces their power over your self-esteem. When you take back your power, the chronic emotions that developed as a reaction will start to fade. Some of these emotions are fear, depression, anger, frustration, or apathy (blocked emotions). In this next activity, you'll learn to monitor your current negative self-talk.

KEEPING TRACK

Materials
  Journal and felt pens

Activity
  1. On a double-page spread in your journal, write down all the put-down messages you send to yourself at this time in your life. List these on the left-hand side, using your *dominant hand.*
  2. Reread each of the messages. On the opposite page across from each one, write down the emotions that come up when you read that message. Use your *nondominant hand.*

3. On a new page, tell the Inner Critic how you really feel about being talked to in this negative way. Let your Inner Child speak by writing with your *nondominant hand.* You don't have to be polite. Do be truthful. Then, write out what you will and will not tolerate from the Critical Parent within. Use your *dominant hand* for this.

4. In your everyday life, watch for the self-critical voice in your head. You may notice that you are feeling tired, cranky, or depressed, and that some negative self-talk is behind your mood. When you notice it, just be aware of it. You may want to do a journal dialogue with it.

Example:

You're worthless	Anger
You're not lovable.	Hurt
You're headed for disaster.	Fear
You're a troublemaker.	Resentment
You will never achieve anything in your life.	Hopelessness
You don't deserve to live.	Helplessness

After rereading the messages *(nondominant hand)*:

I'm really sick and tired of hearing you talk to me as if I were still a naughty little kid. I hate it. Stop it! Now!

Dominant hand:

You are on automatic. You just keep whispering these terrible things in my head and it is not helpful. It makes me tired and depressed, like when I am around my mother, who still talks to me like this. I'm going to be watching you when you start running off at the mouth (in my head), and tell you to stop. You can use your critical abilities in other areas of my life, like correcting reports, etc., but I want you to stop putting me down.

Changing your mind about feelings

In addition to examining and changing self-defeating beliefs about yourself, it is also important to look at your judgments of certain feelings. A child who is taught that big boys don't cry and a lady never gets mad is programmed to judge certain emotions as unacceptable or unbecoming to someone of his or her gender, race, class, economic level, religion, etc. As we have seen in earlier chapters, the offending emotions don't go away. They just go underground.

What we resist persists. When we are taught to avoid and judge a certain feeling, it's easy to get trapped in that emotion or in its opposite. We chronically respond to life from that feeling state, or we mask it. The rage-aholic who is afraid of weakness and vulnerability responds to everything with anger. A temper tantrum feels comfortable and more powerful. What it usually hides are feelings of vulnerability like fear, sadness, or grief.

WHAT I BELIEVE ABOUT FEELINGS

Materials
  Journal and felt pens

Activity
  1. In your journal, make a list of the beliefs you were taught about emotions as you were growing up. Use your *nondominant hand*. Which emotions were okay to express? Which ones weren't?
  2. On the next page, make a list of the difficult or uncomfortable feelings you most often feel today.

Example:
  Beliefs I learned about emotions:
    Don't feel emotions. Be rational.

Emotions make you weak.

Emotions are life threatening.

A man does not feel emotions.

Feelings I feel most now:

Fear

Observation:

What I am afraid of is emotions. As a man, I was brainwashed into thinking I shouldn't feel.

The only way out is to connect myself with my emotions; to discover them and let them into my life; to give them the place and the space they deserve; to welcome my emotions with an open heart.

Applying the mask-making techniques from Chapter Nine can be a powerful and highly effective way to face up to feelings that make you uncomfortable. These can be emotions that you have or that others express, but which make you uneasy or downright afraid.

FACING FEELINGS

Materials

Large brown paper grocery bag, crayons, felt pens and markers, (Optional: oil pastels, collage materials), journal and felt pens

Activity

1. Make a paper bag mask by drawing a face that expresses the emotion you are most afraid of or uncomfortable with.
2. Look at the finished mask and write down your reaction to it. Then give the mask a name. Afterward, give the mask a voice by letting it write with your *nondominant hand* in your journal.

- If it could talk, what would the mask say to you?
- What does it have to teach you or give you?

Christian decided to face up to the emotion of anger by making an angry mask. He then did the drawing shown earlier entitled "At the Mercy of a Dark and Evil Force."

This mask shows the face at the depth of my worst nightmare. It is an angry mask, a rageful face. These are feelings I feared most.

At first the drawing scared him and he didn't like it. However, by putting the image of rage out in front of him in a drawing and looking at it, he discovered that he no longer cowered in its presence.

As a child he had been overwhelmed by his father's rageful outbursts. As an adult, Christian now realized that he had the ability to bring this past trauma out of the depths of his memories into present reality so he could heal himself. In a private session we did some movement work with the drawing of his angry father and of himself as a frightened child. I asked Christian to assume the gesture of the cowering child in the picture. He dropped to the floor on his knees in an almost fetal position. As if protecting himself from harm, he put his right (dominant) hand over his head and his left arm and hand across his midsection.

Guiding him through a meditation with his eyes closed, I asked Christian to visualize a white light of protection around him like the clean white paper that surrounded the small, vulnerable child in his drawing. I then suggested that as an adult he was now free to grow like a plant and emerge up into the light. At this point, Christian started slowly unfurling like a leaf. He created a lovely dance, growing up from the ground until he rose up in a beautiful elongated posture. He cradled an imaginary Inner Child in his arms in a gesture that expressed a Nurturing Parent. Then he allowed his arms to gently fall by his sides, taking the stance of a Protective Parent with great strength and grace.

Afterward Christian said he felt a new sense of self-assurance and of being at peace with his self. "I felt that I had a shield of light and was totally protected by it," Christian shared. "After a while I didn't need to cuddle the Inner Child in my arms because he felt my strength and knew he was protected."

BALANCING FEELINGS

Materials
Floor space to do some movement, journal and felt pens

Activity
1. Take one of your drawings or a mask that depicts feelings that are difficult for you. Perhaps it is an emotion you've been taught not to express or one that frightens you when others express it.
2. Look at the artwork for a while, then allow yourself to assume a posture, facial expression, or gesture that conveys this emotion. Let your body move in any way it wants in order to give full expression to this emotion.
3. Imagine yourself feeling the opposite emotion, one that is comfortable and strengthening for you. Perhaps you started with sadness and then thought about joy, or you went from vulnerability to strength.

   In your mind, visualize what it would feel like to have this new emotion. Use your imagination. What might take you from the first emotion to the second? Do you need protection, energy, nurturing?
4. Do a physical movement or dance that takes you from the first emotion to the second. Start with a gesture or posture that embodies the first feeling. Then move until you find a posture that expresses the second emotion.

5. Draw a picture of the new emotion you got in touch with using your *nondominant hand.* Write about how you moved from one to the other using your *dominant hand.*

- How did you make it safe for yourself to express this new emotion?
- How do you feel now?

Letting your feelings be your guide: changing your life creatively

When you've identified the source of negative self-talk—your Critical Parent within— and also strengthened the Nurturing and Protective Parent within, you have the tools to clear obstacles that are blocking your true fulfillment. But how do you measure fulfillment? Through your feelings. You desire joy or love or peace or contentment. You want to feel creative or enthusiastic or any number of enjoyable emotions. You wish for happiness.

Most people usually lose sight of the feeling state they want and get hung up on the means to that end. We say we want a new car, when what we really want is a new feeling about getting around in the world. Perhaps the old car is always breaking down. Desiring a new car might be our way of saying "I want to feel more secure and comfortable. A new car will be more dependable. It will put my mind at ease. I won't have to worry about it breaking down. And it will be more comfortable to drive." These are all feelings and experiences we want. The car is simply a means to that end. In a similar way, wanting a life partner or a spouse could be our way of saying "I want to feel more love in my life. I want to feel loved and I also want to feel love for another."

You can create the life you want by focusing on the feelings you want and then picturing the realization of your dreams through the use of magazine-photo collages. This is a form of productive daydreaming for fulfilling your fondest wishes. The important thing to keep in mind is the feeling state that you hope to experience. Without that, you may get the thing or person you want but may not feel good after you have them. Why? Because you didn't really know how you wanted to *feel*. Here is an activity to help you focus on the feeling or experience you want.

USING YOUR IMAGINATION

Materials
    Journal and felt pens, art paper, and collage materials

Activity

1. In your journal, write an inventory of your current life. Which aspects of your life would you like to change? What parts of your life feel uncomfortable, restricted, un-fulfilling, or painful? Look at all aspects of your life:

    - finances
    - health
    - relationships
    - home
    - career
    - hobbies
    - other

2. Choose one area of your life where you want to make changes. Create a magazine-photo collage of this area. Picture it the way you would like it to be. Create a visual affirmation of how you would like to feel in relation to this theme. What do the feelings look like? Picture them with photographs.
3. Put your collage up on the wall so you can see it on a regular basis.
4. Imagine the aspect of your personality that is expressing in this collage of how you want things to be. What part of you wants to come out now?

- Is it your Inner Artist?
- Your Business Manager?
- Your Inner Child?
- Your Lover?

5. In your journal, using your *nondominant hand,* let this subpersonality write in the present tense as if it is already expressing itself in your life. This is a new scenario in your life. You can do this with as many areas of your life that are calling for change.

Change does not always have to be prompted by pain. It also can come from your imagination and the Creative Self who guides your growth and expansion into new experiences. If you'd really like to delve deeply into your heart's desires and bring them out in your life, you might want to work with my book *Visioning: Ten Steps to Designing the Life of Your Dreams.* It includes collage, journaling, and more for getting in touch with your Creative Self and learning to follow its guidance in manifesting your true desires. It also provides tools for dealing with creative blocks.

The following activity will help you use your imagination in living your life. By focusing on the feelings you want to have and the qualities you'd like to develop in yourself, the way is cleared for embracing a fully satisfying life.

WRITING A NEW SCRIPT

Materials
Journal and felt pens, collage materials

Activity

1. In your journal, using your *nondominant hand,* write a description of the kind of life you would like to have. Emphasize the emotions and character traits you would

like to foster in this new life. Perhaps you want peace of mind, enthusiasm, creativity, joy.

2. On the next few journal pages, draw or make photo collages depicting the aspects of your personality that are associated with these emotions or traits.

- What do these subpersonalities look like?
- How do they feel?
- What do they need?

3. Write dialogues with these subpersonalities.

- What do they like to do?
- What do they have to offer you?
- How can they enrich your life?
- What do they need from you?

Christian, the man who worked with fear and anger through mask making, drawing, and movement, also did some powerful Voice Dialogue and collage work. In his Voice Dialogue session, an Inner Artist came out who wanted to be honored and allowed to express in Christian's life. I suggested that he allow this Inner Artist to create a collage of how he would like Christian's life to be. His collage is on page 234.

After seeing the collage, I suggested that Christian do some journal dialogues with each aspect of the picture. He used his dominant hand to ask the questions and his nondominant hand to respond for the images in the collage. After each dialogue, he thanked the image. On the next page are some highlights from his journal dialogues in the order in which they were written.

The lower right-hand image (a person chest-high in water with gold and red fish leaping around the shoulders, superimposed over a photograph of water) identified itself as Born from Water with the Earth's Power. It said:

I'm one with water, earth, connected with the sky. From the depths of the ocean to the light. I was born on the night of a full moon. My heart is protected

by the wild salmon. My journey takes me across vast spaces of rivers and seas. From the place of my origin back to the place of my origin. Our journey is protected by the life-giving water, the white light, the universal wisdom. The warmth of Mother Earth flows through our veins. I am your wisdom. Within me I hold everything you will need for your life. Trust me . . . as your inner guide through life. Trust me. You will find me in moments of stillness within yourself. I'm emerging out of your inner subconscious.

Christian continued, letting each image in the collage speak through journal writing. Here is what he said about the experience:

This collage gave me a complete manual of how to live. It didn't give me concrete answers but showed me the way to them. It is a guidebook, so that whenever I get lost I can look at this collage and contemplate it. What is this section saying? What is that image telling me? It's sort of a personal bible.

It was fascinating to pick images at random, yet when I started dialoguing with them I could see that each picture was in exactly the right place. Each image had its own precise meaning. It shows that there are no coincidences. Everything fits together. This collage is the image of my life. After I did this collage I painted a watercolor seascape portraying my experiences of sunsets over the ocean. It was the first time I had painted in about thirty years, since I was a schoolboy.

It was an experiment—trying to take my feelings about sunsets I had recently seen and photographed, and put them onto paper with paint and color. I wanted to express the Inner Artist I had encountered in the Voice Dialogue session with Lucia. This was the Inner Artist's way of coming out. I was very pleased. For a first watercolor, it was great. I just went for it, and the Inner Critic was hardly present.

Christian then created a collage titled "The Boys Having a Good Time" (see page 236). Here are his comments about that collage:

This really expresses the feelings of having a good time. When I started it, I wanted to do one with words only. But when I saw the photo of the three little boys, I just had to use it. I was using more of an artistic touch in making this piece: the colors, the design. The letters felt like dice which I had thrown, and they landed randomly at their own whim. The collage says, Joy. Happiness. No worries. It's my Inner Child who loves to play and fool around and be together with others.

The next thing Christian did was to take a two-week vacation in Hawaii, a place that contains all the images he had put in his collage. He honored his Inner Artist (photographer and painter) by taking plenty of film and art supplies to paint pictures of his inner experiences.

From a cowering child of the past to a powerful man who has found his creative powers buried deep within, Christian's story is a hero's journey of self-discovery through creative expression. It led to a career change and a new life.

It is my hope that you, too, will embark on your own adventure to find the Holy Grail of your own Creative Self. Follow your feelings, paint them, write them, dance them, sing them. Live your life out loud. Live your life with feeling.

In a group art workshop, Christian created this collage of boys having fun.

RESOURCES

Materials

All Chapters

• Journal (8½" x 11")

You can use a larger or smaller journal, but I find that this size is optimal. It accommodates both drawing and collage as well as writing.

Hardback journals can be purchased in bookstores, stationery stores, and art supply stores. In art supply stores they are usually called sketcher's diaries and come with hardback covers. In bookstores they come with a variety of covers, including cloth and leather binding. Avoid the ones with lots of borders, inscriptions, and decorations on the page. This is *your* journal, a place to express your own creativity.

Your choice of one of the following:

- Blank hardbound book with blank unlined pages (my personal preference)
- Spiral sketch pad with white unlined paper
- A sturdy paperback journal with white unlined paper
- Three-ring folder with white unlined paper
- Felt pens (twelve colors or more) with fine tip for writing
- Felt markers (twelve colors or more) with wide tip for drawing

Chapter Three

- Crayons or oil pastels (twelve colors or more)
- Drawing paper, white (18" x 24", or approximately 12" x 18")
  White sulphite drawing paper, 80 lb. You'll need a paper that is heavy and absorbent enough for felt pen, crayon, and pastel drawing as well as painting (in later chapters). See below in the Sources for Art Materials and Supplies section for art and craft suppliers who carry this paper. Similar paper can also be purchased in large art pads at art supply stores. Appropriate uses and media are usually designated on the cover of the pad.

Chapter Four

- Drawing paper and plain newsprint paper (18" x 24")
- Chalk pastels in assorted colors (preferably twelve or more)
- Spray fixative or hairspray (to prevent pastel drawings from rubbing off)
- Box of watercolor paints and brushes (tubes or colors in pans)
  If tubes are used, a palette for mixing the paints will be needed. Small inexpensive ones are available through art suppliers. They have indentations for mixing water and paint and come in plastic, tin, or ceramic.
- Optional: Colored art paper (12" x 18") for drawing and painting, such as Strathmore colored art paper pads, 300 series
- Jar of water
- Magazines with lots of photos and visual images
- Colored paper for collage (such as construction paper, origami paper, etc.)

- Scissors
- Glue
- Paper towels
- Trash container
- Smock, old shirt, or apron
- Sound system for playing recorded music
- Recorded music: your own collection or music recommended in the chapter
- *Music for the Mozart Effect, Volume III,* recordings compiled by Don Campbell

Chapter Five

- Red clay (air-drying self-hardening red clay, such as Laguna EM 207 or comparable) available in 25-lb. blocks in a plastic bag. Gray or red terra cotta clay can also be used. Both are available in art, craft, or ceramic supply stores.
- Work surface (wood, Masonite, heavy cardboard, or tabletop with plastic cover)
- Heavy piece of string or twine for cutting clay from the block
- Bowl of warm water
- Plastic airtight container for storing smaller pieces of clay (like storage refrigerator)

Chapter Six

- Sound system for playing recorded music
- Recorded music: your own or music recommended in the chapter
- *Music for the Mozart Effect* by Don Campbell
- CD set: *The Sound of Feelings* by Jessie Allen Cooper
- Art supplies as listed for earlier chapters

Chapter Seven

- Sound system for playing recorded music
- Recorded music: your own collection or music recommended in the chapter
- Audiotape or CD: *Endless Wave, Volume I* by Gabrielle Roth
- CD set: *The Sound of Feelings* by Jessie Allen Cooper
- Art supplies (as listed in earlier chapters)

Chapter Eight

- Drawing paper, white sulphite (18" x 24", as indicated for Chapter Three)
- Magazines
- Optional: colored paper, such as construction or origami paper
- Scissors
- Glue

Chapter Nine

- Art supplies (as listed for earlier chapters)
- Tempera paint and brushes
- Collage supplies (scissors, white glue—such as Elmer's Glue—and colored paper)
- Plaster mask-making supplies:

    plaster cloth strips (for forming mask)

    Vaseline

    old towels

    paper towels

    plastic drop cloth

- Paper mask-making supplies

    Large brown bags from supermarket for bag masks

    Small jars of tempera paint (six to eight colors) or set of watercolors

    Brush

    Jar of water

    Paper plates or poster board or railroad board

    Fabric stretched over cardboard

- Decorative elements, such as ribbons, colored tissue paper, cellophane, yarn, odds and ends of scrap paper, fabric, feathers, magazine photos, cardboard, construction or heavy art paper, etc.

Chapter Ten
- Journal and felt pens
- Art paper and collage materials

Sources for art materials and supplies

Art Materials
- Your local arts and crafts store, office supply store, or stationer
- Catalogs and E-mail services:

NowGetCreative.com
E-mail: Renee@NowGetCreative.com
Features all my books and audio programs as well my favorite art and journal supplies. Good for one-stop shopping.

Sax Arts & Crafts, New Berlin, WI
www.saxarts.com
Phone: (800) 558-6696

Nasco Arts & Crafts, Plymouth, MN
E-mail: modesto@eNASCO.com
www.eNASCO.com
Phone: (800) 558-9595

For More Advanced Work in Art
Should you want to go on to explore other media (with or without professional instruction), the following suppliers carry a full line of fine art materials.

Artisan/Santa Fe, Inc., Santa Fe, NM
Phone: (800) 331-6375 (Catalog)

Daniel Smith: The Catalogue of Artist's Materials, Seattle, WA
www.danielsmith.com
Phone: (800) 426-6740

Books, audio, and video

Capacchione, Lucia

BOOKS

The Creative Journal: The Art of Finding Yourself
The Creative Journal for Children: A Guide for Parents, Teachers and Counselors
The Creative Journal for Parents
The Creative Journal for Teens
Lighten Up Your Body, Lighten Up Your Life (with Johnson and Strohecker)
The Picture of Health: Healing Your Life with Art
The Power of Your Other Hand
Putting Your Talent to Work (with Peggy Van Pelt)
Recovery of Your Inner Child
Visioning: Ten Steps to Designing the Life of Your Dreams
The Well-Being Journal: Drawing on Your Inner Power to Heal Yourself

AUDIO

The Picture of Health. Well-Being Journal Meditations (CD).
    Available from Lucia Capacchione, Cambria, CA
    www.luciac.com or www.NowGetCreative.com
The Wisdom of Your Other Hand. Five tapes on Creative Journal and art therapy, inner family work, body-mind healing, relationship, career.
    Available from Sounds True
    Phone: (800) 333-9185
    soundstrue.com

Music and Movement

SUGGESTED AUDIOCASSETTES AND CDS

Chidvilasanada, Gurumayi, *The Power of the Mantra.*

> Available from Siddha Yoga Bookstores, South Fallsburg, NY
>
> Phone: (888) 422-3334

Cooper, Jessie Allen, with Lucia Capacchione, *The Sound of Feelings: Music for Emotional Healing.* Series of five CDs with music to evoke the nine Families of Feelings plus an introductory narration by Dr. Capacchione on the art of emotional expression. A sampler CD is also available with one musical composition for each of the nine Families of Feelings.

> Available from Cooper Sound Waves, P.O. Box 5190, Santa Monica, CA 90409
>
> Phone: (310) 392-7784
>
> www.cooperarts.com

Green, Suzin, *Dream Shield Journey.* An inspirational personal spiritual journey in music.

> Available from Suzin Green, Box 572, Kingston, NJ 08528
>
> Phone: (609) 252-9185

Green, Suzin and Sura, *Hearts on Fire.* Devotional music inspired by East Indian traditional chant.

Jones, Michael, *Touch.*

McFerrin, Bobby, *Medicine Man* (the following cuts are used):

> "Medicine Man"
>
> "The 23rd Psalm"
>
> "Common Threads"
>
> "Baby"
>
> "Yes, You"
>
> "Soma so de la de sase"
>
> "Sweet in the Mornin'"

Miller, Radhika, *Sunlit Reverie.* Flute music.

Mozart as compiled by Don Campbell, *Music for the Mozart Effect.*

Volume I, Strength of Mind (to improve intelligence and learning)

Volume II, Heal the Body (for rest and relaxation)

Volume III, Unlock the Creative Spirit (stimulates creativity and imagination)

Nakai, R. Carlos, Native American Flute music. *Canyon Trilogy, Inner Voices, Earth Spirit, Sanctuary, In Beauty We Return.*

Roth, Gabrielle, and the Mirrors. *Endless Wave, Initiation,* and *Trance.*

Roth has many other audio programs suitable for use with movement, art, music and sound making.

Available from Raven Recording

Phone: (800) 76-RAVEN

www.Ravenrecording.com

Satie, Erik. Any piano solo renditions of this French Impressionist composer's work are suitable for meditative drawing, art making, and movement, especially *Trois Gymnopédies.* and *Trois Gnossiennes.*

Scott, Tony, *Music for Yoga Meditation and Other Joys*

Scott, Tony, with Shinchi Yuze and Hozan Yamamoto, *Music for Zen Meditation and Other Joys.* Clarinet, koto, and shakuhachi.

Smith, Thomas, *The Natural Cello.* Gregorian chant and nature sounds.

Available from NorthSound

Phone: (800) 336-5666

Emotional Intelligence

BOOKS

Goleman, Daniel, *Emotional Intelligence* and *Working with Emotional Intelligence.*

Men for Change, *Healthy Relationships: A Violence-Prevention Curriculum.* For information: Andrew Safer, 22 Chappell Street, Dartmouth, Nova Scotia, Canada B3A 3P2.

Phone: (902) 422-8476

E-mail: asafer@eastlink.ca

www.m4c.ns.ca

AUDIO

McLaren, Karla. *Emotional Genius: How Your Emotions Can Save Your Life.* Series of 6 cassettes with booklet.

Available from Sounds True

Phone: (800) 333-9185

www.soundstrue.com

Expressive Arts and Healing

BOOKS

Ganim, Barbara, *Art and Healing*

McNiff, Shaun, *Art as Medicine: Creating a Therapy of the Imagination*

Rogers, Natalie, *The Creative Connection: Expressive Arts as Healing*

Samuels, Michael, and Mary Rockwood Lane, *Creative Healing*

Health and Healing

AUTHORS

The following authors are all quite prolific and have written a veritable library of books on body-mind healing. They have been mentioned earlier in the book, along with titles. Instead of listing the titles here, I am providing their names alphabetically. Any of their nonfiction will be a valuable resource in conjunction with this book.

Benson, Dr. Herbert

Borysenko, Joan

Chopra, Deepak

Cousins, Norman

Dossey, Larry

Northrup, Christiane

Pearsall, Paul

Pelletier, Kenneth

Pennebaker, James

Pert, Candace

Selye, Hans

Siegel, Bernie

The Arts

BOOKS

Drawing

Brookes, Mona

> *Drawing with Children*

> *Drawing for Older Children and Teens*

Edwards, Betty, *Drawing on the Right Side of the Brain*

Cinema

Gurian, Michael, *What Stories Does My Son Need?*

McKee, Robert, *Story Structure*

Solomon, Gary, *The Motion Picture Prescription: Watch This Movie and Call Me in the Morning*

Music

Campbell, Don, *The Mozart Effect*

Hart, Mickey, *Drumming on the Edge of Magic: A Journey into the Spirit of Percussion*

Joseph, Arthur, *The Sound of the Soul*

Ortiz, John M., *The Tao of Music: Sound Psychology*

Instructional Audio and Video

Ashley-Ferrand, Thomas, *Mantra: Sacred Words of Power*

> Audiocassette series containing history and information about mantras.

Available from Sounds True

Phone: (800) 333-9185

www.soundstrue.com

Joseph, Arthur, *Vocal Awareness* audiocassettes (set of six tapes)

Sing Your Heart Out (audiotapes) Vocal Awareness Video

All available from Sounds True

Phone: (800) 333-9185

www.soundstrue.com

Roth, Gabrielle

The Wave Video (tape of a dance workout)

I Dance the Body Electric Video (interview with Gabrielle Roth)

Available from Raven Recording

Phone: (800) 76-RAVEN

www.Ravenrecording.com

Ecstatic Dance: The Wave, The Power Wave, The Inner Wave Videocassette set (3 tapes)

Available from Sounds True

Phone: (800) 333-9185

CREATIVITY

Books

Arrien, Angeles, *The Nine Muses: A Mythological Path to Creativity*

Cameron, Julia, *The Artist's Way* or *The Vein of Gold*

Maisel, Eric, *Fearless Creating*

McNiff, Shaun, *Trust the Process: An Artist's Guide to Letting Go*

Phillips, Jan, *Marry Your Muse: Making a Lasting Commitment to Your Creativity*

Richards, M. C., *Centering: In Pottery, Poetry, and the Person*

Rilke, Rainer Maria, *Letters to a Young Poet*

Rumi, Jelaluddin, *The Essential Rumi*, translations by Coleman Barks with John Moyne

Sark, *The Bodacious Book of Succulence: Daring to Live Your Succulent Wild Life*

Stone, Hal and Sidra, *Embracing Our Selves, Partnering*

STORYTELLING AND WRITING

Books

Cameron, Julia, *The Artist's Way*

Goldberg, Natalie, *Wild Mind: Living the Writer's Life, Writing Down the Bones*

Whyte, David, *The Heart Aroused*

Wooldridge, Susan Goldsmith, *Poemcrazy: Freeing Your Life with Words*

Rilke, Rainer Maria, *Letters to a Young Poet*

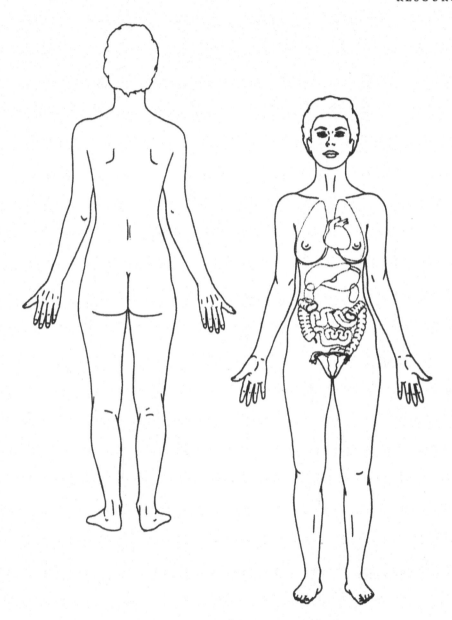

Body Charts: Chapter Three

Note: you may photocopy these charts for repeated use

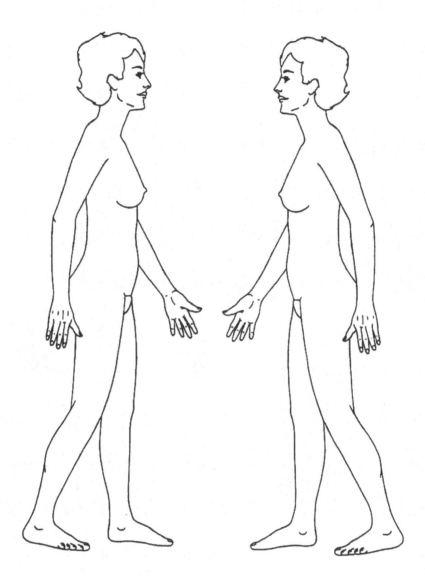

Body Charts: Chapter Three

Note: you may photocopy these charts for repeated use

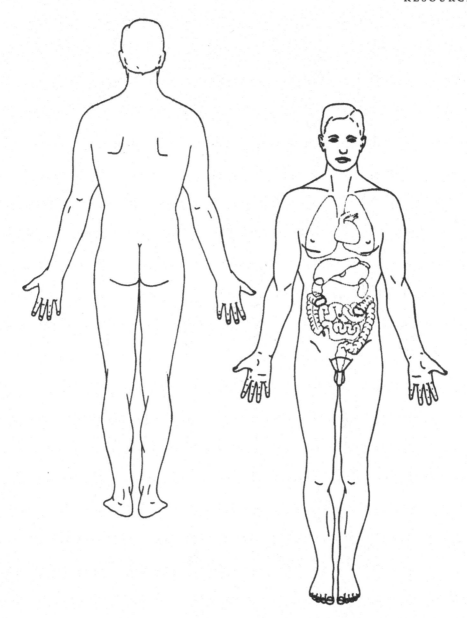

Body Charts: Chapter Three

Note: you may photocopy these charts for repeated use

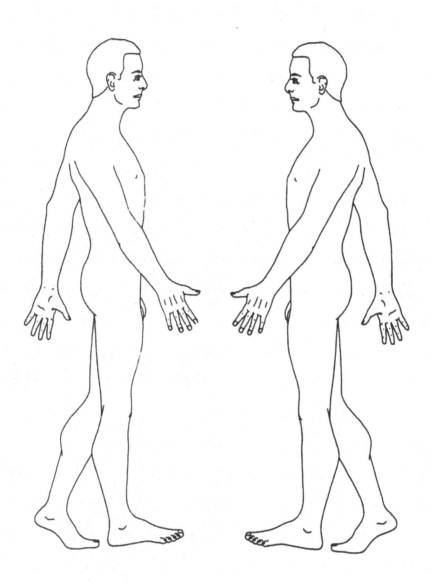

Body Charts: Chapter Three

Note: you may photocopy these charts for repeated use

ABOUT THE AUTHOR

Lucia Capacchione Ph.D., A.T.R., R.E.A.T., is a registered art therapist, artist, popular workshop leader and best-selling author of several classics in the field of expressive arts therapy. A pioneer of Inner Child work and healing through writing and drawing with the non-dominant hand, she trains health care professionals and educators internationally. She has also been a corporate consultant to the Walt Disney Company. Dr. Capacchione is director of the Creative Journal Expressive Arts Certification Training Program. She lives on California's central coast.